Drift

Unmasked

The Legend and The Man

To Lynne,

"Catch the Drift!"

Gibbes McDowell

GIBBES McDOWELL

For Permission requests, write to:

YBR Publishing
c/o J&C Wordsmiths LLC
PO Box 4904
Beaufort SC 29903-4904
contact@ybrpub.com
843-597-0912

DRIFTWOOD UNMASKED

GIBBES McDOWELL

ISBN- 0-9980582-8-9
ISBN-13: 978-0-9980582-8-3

Cover photo - John Wollwerth www.wollwerthimagery.com
Cover mask - Hank Herring
Editor- Bill Barnier www.ybrpub.com
Cover and interior design – Jack Gannon &
        Cyndi Williams-Barnier www.ybrpub.com

DRIFTWOOD UNMASKED

...It was Driftwood's personality that drove him to poke his finger into the eye of conformity...

DRIFTWOOD UNMASKED

DEDICATION

This book, a work of fiction based on real life, is dedicated to a man locally known as Driftwood Cory. An iconic character, Driftwood lived in a world of his own creation by the beach, eking out a living selling driftwood art, horseshoe crab masks, and odd collectibles by his own hand. He was an eccentric, mysterious Irish rogue. Not much was known of the real Cory; some say he was AWOL from the British Navy, or a bagman for the Irish Republican Army (IRA) living under an alias. Others say he just washed up on a high tide. This fictional story weaves a tale of "what ifs" and "maybes" around the backdrop of a host of characters, typically found in small Southern coastal towns of the early 20th century.

This story is also dedicated…

…To unique characters from small towns across the America of our youth who made our towns so special. Mayberry had its Barney Fife and Earnest T. Bass. Beaufort, South Carolina had Driftwood Cory…

…To life's underdogs, still fighting for their equal seat at the table of life. Oppressed by the powerful, dismissed by most, with a little luck, and a pinch of divine intervention, they win the day. …

…and especially to members of our armed forces still fighting wars, present and past, living through the pain of Post-Traumatic Stress Disorder (PTSD). Driftwood's fictionalized life in these pages and the postscript chapter, "Channeling Driftwood", express deep empathy for those whose lives are forever disfigured by the horrors of war. Before PTSD there was "shell shock".

Driftwood's life story, both fictionalized and real, is a blend of both.

The Gullah culture is alive and well on Saint Helena Island, South Carolina, and on the surrounding islands where this story is set. The Gullah language in this book has been respectfully translated from "Gullah Fuh Oonuh, A Guide to the Gullah Language" by Virginia Mixon Geraty, as well as various other reliable resources. The fictional characters are heavily vested in the traditions passed down from the generations living where the story takes place.

DRIFTWOOD UNMASKED

A steady rain drummed on the corrugated tin roof, fogging the windows of the gray cinder block office building. In the corner, atop a musty oak whiskey barrel, sat the old RCA Victor AM/FM radio crackling out a lonesome Jimmy Dean tune.

"Every morning at the mine you could see him arrive.

He stood six-foot-six and weighed two-forty-five.

Kinda broad at the shoulder

And narrow at the hip

And everybody knew you didn't give no lip to big John.

Big John, big John...

Big bad John."

"Sheriff! I got the County Cemetery on the line. Somebody's tried to dig up old 'Driftwood' again."

The sheriff, deeply engrossed in drafting his bridge dedication address, snapped back, "Damn that guy. Took me 30 years to get that ornery old Mick in the ground the first time. He wasn't worth two cents alive, and not half that dead."

Newly promoted young Deputy Thad Rollins turned away from the phone.

"I guess old legends die hard, Sheriff. You can be pretty sure it wasn't anyone from the islands though, 'cause o' those little root bags always showing up on his grave. Ain't nobody who knows gonna take that chance."

"Big John, big John..."

Turning back to the phone, Rollins asked, "Who did you say you are? From where?... Sheriff, I—"

"Not now, Rollins. Can't you see I'm busy?"

"I think you really need to take this one, Sheriff."

Charging to the deputy's desk, the sheriff stuck out his hand and took the phone. "Gimme that... Hello?... Who?... The hell you say!"

"Everybody knew it was the end of the line for big John

Big John, big John

Big bad John..."

CHAPTER I
A Rule of Three

In the study of numerology, three can be the number of time: Past, Present, and Future; of Birth, Life, Death; Beginning, Middle, End. The number three was considered sacred in many religions. For Christians it was the divine number, as in The Holy Trinity. Three was considered The Lucky Number, "third time lucky". It was the magical number of fairy tales with heroes facing three tasks. The Pythagoreans taught that the number three was the first true number. Three was the first number that formed a geometrical figure - the triangle ...

Year 1569

Near the island of Tortuga, a Spanish galleon, loaded with coin stamped from looted Inca gold, ran aground while seeking shelter from a hurricane. The island, discovered by Christopher Columbus in 1492, was so-named because it looked from afar like the shell of a turtle, or Tortuga in Spanish. Located just north of Haiti, Tortuga became a neutral hideout for pirates raiding up and down the Caribbean. The political rivalries between the Spanish, French, English, and Dutch fighting for control of the island created the legal limbo attractive to those seeking to live life on their own terms.

The good life of pirating came to an end in the Caribbean in 1684 with the Treaty of Ratisbon. Signed by the European powers, it forbade sailing under foreign flags, thereby effectively ending state-sponsored piracy. The surviving pirates fled north, beyond control of the Spanish, British, and French navies, to the South Carolina coast.

In 1684 it was one of those ships, the *Esmeralda*, which found itself foundering in a July hurricane at night in the surf of an unknown island. In her hold had been spirited three wooden chests not listed on the ship's manifest, the last legacy of a betrayed pirate captain left dangling from the king's gallows on Tortuga. The *Esmeralda*'s new captain and key lieutenants intended an early retirement from piracy beyond the king's reach, unbeknownst to their crew.

Measuring 140 feet in length, 32 feet at her beam and weighing in at 150 tons, the captured merchant ketch *Esmeralda* was a pirate's dream boat. She was shallow-drafted to work coastal waters and inlets and furled enough sail to make her fast and maneuverable, perfect for hit-and-run profiteering. A scavenged twenty-pound parrot gun was mounted on her bow, and two pair of forty-pounders port and starboard. She had enough firepower to "stand and board" her victims, but not enough to go muzzle-to-muzzle with Her Majesty's big gun ships. It was better to outrun the gallows through narrow channels and shallow bays than stand and fight.

The crew of the *Esmeralda*, long experienced with the Caribbean, had no reliable charts for their new heading. Relying instead on years under sail, they felt safe staying offshore to avoid dangerous sandbars known to haunt the many sounds and inlets of the South Carolina coast, and close enough for the mast-watch to barely make out the headland. They headed toward a deep-water sound rumored to safely host the occasional privateer. Their intended port of call was Port Royal, South Carolina.

The unsettled weather that had been following the *Esmeralda* northward began to find its footing. Three days out of Tortuga, lashing squalls turned into the front wall of a hurricane. The ship's captain tried to outrun the storm, but without proper charts, he overshot the safety of Port Royal Sound. A sudden gust snapped the main mast, jumbled rope and tackle fell astern, fouling the ship's rudder and leaving the *Esmeralda* unable to steer, and helpless to her fate.

Hard aground in a pounding surf, the *Esmeralda*'s timbers snapped and groaned. Terrified sailors screamed as lightning flashed in thunderous bolts, lighting the chaos in kaleidoscopic relief. A cold stinging rain lashed the decks. Bam, bam, bam, the relentless surf pounded the ship against the sandbar. Half a mile offshore the *Esmeralda* shuddered her final death groan and split at her keel, spilling flailing men into the cold dark sea. Swallowed in the darkness and tossed by ten-foot waves, most of the sailors drowned with screams of terror sounding in the night.

Only six survived. Daybreak found them washed up into the dune line, barely-alive flotsam from the storm's rage. About them lay the broken bones of their ship. Along the beach the corpses of their fellow pirates were scattered among the wreckage.

One of the survivors, First Mate Shaun O'Neal, called the other survivors around him. They were a shaken bunch, with a lost, stunned look in their eyes. Boson's mate Jonas Cox nursed a twisted ankle, while Jeb Ames, 15-year-old cabin boy, wrapped a bloody gash in another sailor's right arm. Shipwright Christopher "Jonesy" Jones slumped over a palmetto log, lightly sobbing, shaking his head side to side as if trying to shake himself into a different reality than the one before him. The other two men, ship's rigger Cyrus Mills, and a deck hand, stared at the sand, waiting for someone to tell them what to do.

"Gather up, lads. I count six head. It's a sorry lot we've drawn, but if we all pull together we can survive this beachin'," said O'Neal.

O'Neal could make out the carcass of the *Esmeralda* offshore, lying broken on the sandbar that killed her. As troubled men often do in a crisis, they rallied around the one who exuded the confidence they needed to survive. Above average in height, square rigged of barreled chest, with broad shoulders and powerful arms was Shaun O'Neal. His light blue eyes, which mirrored the color of the sea, had a calming effect on all he met. The survivors ceded command to him. Former First Mate Shaun O'Neal was now Captain.

"Mates, the first thing we need to do is build a right sturdy raft from some of this wreckage and make for the *Esmeralda* before the next tide finishers 'er off.

Maybe we can salvage some food from the hold and some guns. I got no idea where we are. Food, guns, and shelter are what we need first, an' ere's to 'opin' there be some water about this God forsaken place."

They began the solemn task of unraveling rope and lumber from the carnage on the beach.

Jonas Cox turned, limping on his bad ankle. "Cap'n, what about our mates? We can't just leave 'em like this, can we?"

"They'll be no deader on the next tide than the last. If you don't want to join 'em, we best look to ourselves first. We can give 'em a proper burial on the morrow."

The makeshift raft reached the *Esmeralda* mid-morning. The wind was fresh, the seagulls already eyeing the odd bits of food and shiny objects around the wreck. The smell of death had already begun to seep from the pores of the once proud ship.

"Scatter about mates. Salvage what you can."

They accounted for eight muskets, powder and shot, some sail cloth, hand tools, basic cooking utensils, and a barrel of biscuits and salt pork.

Jonesy shouted out from deep within the hold, "Cap'n O'Neal, look what's been a-hidin' 'neath our very noses this 'ole voyage. That sorry barnacle of a captain never told us we was carrying treasure! Dirty scoundrel was 'olding out on us. Serves him right to be with the fishes, it does."

"Jonesy, what're you 'ollering about down there?"

"Cap'n, come, 'ave a looksee."

Captain Shaun O'Neal peered through a split in the decking to see Jonesy fighting the lock on one of three large oak chests, each double strapped with iron banding.

"What makes you think it's treasure?"

"Well, Cap'n, me an' the crew didn't board 'em, an' theren't no clothes locker needin' locks and iron strappins such as these, is there? And it's heavier than a dead 'orse, it is."

Captain O'Neal gathered the men around the chest and handed one a heavy hammer from the shipwright's forge. "Give her a smart whack with this, Jeb."

All eyes followed the cabin boy's hammer blow and gave a shout when the lock popped and dropped heavily to the floor.

"Open her up, Jonesy," implored one.

"What ya waiting for?" added another.

Captain O'Neal gave Jonesy the nod. The rusty hinges creaked with unaccustomed use, but the heavy lid opened to the morning sunshine filtering through the wreck.

There was dead silence.

With quickened breath and trembling, calloused hands, the pirates ran their grimy fingers through the elbow-deep cache of gold Spanish coin. Double-cupped hands scooped up and spilled waterfalls of pirates' dreams, the clinking ring of untold wealth sending shivers up the men's spines. Gleaming in the morning sun and fresh as the day they were stamped at the Spanish mint in Peru, the newfound "Escudos", or doubloons as they came to be called, claimed the soul of every eye.

Captain O'Neal rubbed his hands together and nodded to all about the chest of gold opines.

"I'm guessing there was more to our old cap'n's 'angin' on Tortuga than meets the eye, by the look 'o this 'ere treasure."

Jonesy could hardly contain himself. "An' there's two more chests Cap'n! Open the others. Let's see."

"Hold fast mates, the tide's a-risin'. The *Esmeralda* won't stand another night in this surf. We have to get everything we can back to the beach. You two, give a heft to those other two chests. Are they as heavy as this first?"

"Aye Cap'n, they's all four-man 'eavy."

"Let's get 'em topside. Jonesy, Cyrus, rig us a hoist. Span the hold with yonder busted main beam. There's block and tackle aplenty layin' about to do yer liftin' for ye. We'll dump a cannon and use the wheeled gun carriage to roll the treasure across the sand bar to the raft. Jonas, Jeb, you two walk out front to find a hard-packed pathway to the raft. Spud her hard and sound, lads. Once topside we'll re-rig tackle and rope from deck to raft to do our pullin' fer us. We can't afford to founder now, so close to this golden salvation. This treasure'll buy no rum an' tarts 'ere, but we can damn sure come back and fetch her later, when we've the wind at our backs."

On white topped swells, the six surviving pirates rowed their salvaged provisions and treasure chests through a slough in the beach, riding the incoming tide up a small tidal creek behind their island. Around several bends they rowed, toward a forested peninsula of high ground, marked on its southernmost end with the sun-dried, salt-cured skeleton of a giant oak tree. The souls of Inca dead tolled the sailors in tortured sinews and beaded sweat, spent hauling blood money to another resting place.

"Put your backs into it, mates!"

"A fine marker if ever there was one," remarked Captain O'Neal. "We'll make camp 'ere and bury the chests un'er this old tree."

The first night on the beach was as miserable a night as could be imagined. At dusk, swarms of mosquitoes sought blood from every exposed inch of flesh. The men were hot, thirsty, hungry, and scared. Strange haunting sounds could be heard from the dense underbrush beyond the dunes; perhaps tortured imaginations longing for daybreak?

Dawn was long in coming and not before they succumbed to spending the balance of the night waist deep in the surf, arms locked into a protective circle, dousing the incessant waves of biting insects with alternating waves of salt water.

The first order of the next morning was burial duty. Twenty-three comrades were laid to rest in shallow graves some fifty yards up into the dune field, between ocean and forest. Few words were spared for the dead. Captain O'Neal led off with a Sailor's Prayer; all removing their caps in solemn respect.

"No more a watch to stand, my friends.

For you are drifting on an ebbing tide.

Eight bells has rung, Dog watch is done.

A new berth waits you on the other side."

Silent lips moved in unison as the last shovel of sand was thrown into the mass grave. All other energy was saved for the challenge of building shelter from weather and bugs before the coming nightfall.

A flat spot to build upon was found above the tideline and far enough from the woods and dunes to offer a soothing breeze. It was roughly framed by four palmetto trees, squaring approximately twelve feet by twelve feet.

Captain O'Neal organized the men into two work details. Jonesy, the *Esmeralda*'s shipwright, and Cyrus, the rigger, were tasked with construction, while the others were sent to find the raw materials for the job.

"Build us a fittin' shelter from this God-forsaken Hell," encouraged O'Neil.

A driftwood ridgepole was tied ten feet high between two trees. Side poles were equally spaced seven feet high along both sides. Across this basic frame was stretched a cover of sailcloth for the roof and side walls. Another section of sailcloth made a ground cover within. Initially, bedding was piles of cut palmetto fronds, offering some cushion from the packed, gritty beach sand. Basic tables and chairs were fashioned of lumber scraps from the wreck, along with favorably formed pieces of natural driftwood. A small, steady creosote fire, built of driftwood pine knots laid at the shelter entrance, provided a smoke screen against the biting flies. Day three found the surviving pirates reasonably secure in spirit and shelter.

The marooned pirates survived for three months on biscuits and pork, supplementing their diet with shellfish dug from the salt marsh creek behind the island and fresh water found in a cattail pond further inland. They walked the length of their island searching for any resources that could enhance their chances for survival.

The island measured about three miles long and one-half mile wide at its midpoint. Just at the limit of their vision, north and south, they could see the faint outline of other islands. Behind their island was a vast marsh extending far to the west to another distant tree line. Be it island or headland, they did not know. They found no other sign of humankind on the island; no fire pits, no dwellings, no sign of the ax.

Life as castaways became a simple routine of waking to the morning surf and walking the beach to see what fate had sent to them on the night's tide. Sometimes it was a piece of rope or lumber they could use in their makeshift shelter. Sometimes a particularly rough sea would bring a beached fish or dolphin. Real meat was hard to come by; they tired of the occasional raccoon treed in the dense maritime forest behind the beach. Lifelong sailors all, the pirates had an innate fear of going too deep into the woods. The near-fatal strike of a large rattlesnake, while cabin boy Jeb Ames was gathering firewood along the tree line, gave credence to this fear, as did Bosons' mate Jonas Cox being treed for half a day by a wild boar. Strange, shrieking screams in the deep nighttime jungle kept tensions high. They were wary of what else might be lurking in there for a luckless sailor. They preferred the open safety of the beach. Twice though, the men captured a giant sea turtle, come ashore to lay its eggs, and feast they did. They learned to find turtle nests by following the three-foot wide crawling tracks in the sand as roadmaps to nests built in the night. Ghost crabs, discarding empty turtle eggshells from their burrows, revealed where to dig for hidden nests and fresh-hatched baby turtles. The soft baby turtles made for a crispy morsel when skewered and fire roasted. Survival it was, but at the cost of a gruesome lesson hard learned. It was the sudden appearance of dozens of ghost crab burrows above their buried mates that gave them pause. Tattered pieces of a sailor's shirt, a belt buckle, and shoelace mixed with other beach litter showed the pirates how the industrious ghost crabs could dig for their dinner.

It was their daily routine and small thankful gifts of fate that kept hope alive for the stranded pirates. They considered building a raft and taking their chances at sea. But they had no charts, no directions, and no assurance that the next island, or the next, would fare them any better than the one they were on. No, it was decided they would build a signal fire to the first mast spotted and risk the lifesaving lie that they were merchant sailors put adrift by pirates. They would then lay low for a couple of months before putting out to recover their buried treasure.

Boredom was a constant companion to the stranded pirates. Watch duty fell into complacency. After daily tasks, they would gamble and play checkers with Spanish doubloons on wooden barrel tops. Their seventh surviving and silent shipmate, Greed, rarely raised a voice among them. As time wore on and the hope of rescue waned, the once all-consuming power of gold faded; coins became mere baubles.

On a morning beach walk, as was the custom every morning, the sailors came upon foot prints in the sand. Human foot prints, barefoot prints, and lots of them! Maybe two dozen or more, half washed out by the night's tide. Whomever made them had beached at high water. Skid marks, such as those made by dragging a small boat or skiff, led out of sight into the thick jungle.

Jonas Cox cupped his hands to his mouth to shout out to the newcomers but was hushed by Jonesy.

"Let's not be to 'asty 'afore we find out who these chaps are. Quick mates, back to camp an' put out the campfire. The Cap'n will know what to do."

Their fire smoke had already been seen from the other end of the island. The pirates weren't the only refugees from the Spanish empire. A band of Indians, fleeing slave hunters in Spanish Florida, had moved north, too, hopping from island to island by dugout canoe, hunting and fishing their way to freedom.

The Spanish enslavement of native peoples began in the Antilles by the greatest Spanish slaver in history and heroic discoverer of America, Christopher Columbus. The Spanish colonists used slavery and production quotas to force the local labor to bring a return on expedition and colonization investments. Thousands died in forced labor camps while growing crops and searching for gold. The introduction of European diseases took its toll on native populations, reducing them by ninety percent over several decades. In 1537, the Papacy in Spain officially banned slavery in the West Indies. This ruling had little effect in mainland colonies where subjugation under the name of *"repartimiento"*, or labor for protection, persisted until Spain lost its grip in the New World. Spanish slavers from St. Augustine, Florida continued to hunt and sell native peoples into slavery until Spain ceded Spanish Florida to the United States in 1819.

To the Timucua Indians who landed on the marooned pirates' island, the camp fire at the other end of the island was surely a sign of pursuing slavers. Ambush and murder was afoot. The night after discovering the foot prints on the other end of the island, Pirate Captain Shaun O'Neal gathered his crew around a council fire to decide the best plan of action.

"Lads, load your muskets with round shot and keep your sabers at hand. Jeb, you keep a lookout from that dune top yonder and holler out at anything that moves. Cyrus will relieve you at daybreak."

"We'll go have us a looksee at these newcomers in the full morning sunshine from the open beach at low tide. With the water at our backs we'll not be having any surprises."

In the flickering light of a dying campfire the pirates nestled down into a restless slumber. Their crude palmetto and canvas bedding offered little solace against the coming morning. Hours passed with no visitors, save a cautious raccoon scavenging the beach for his dinner. Young cabin boy Jeb Ames, fighting to keep his eyes open against the lolling sound of a rolling surf, bolted upright at a nearby sudden sound, like that of a single string pick of a guitar. Eyes wide open he stared speechless at the feathered arrow shaft protruding from his chest. Silent bodies crept past his still twitching corpse to surround the sleeping pirate camp.

An early morning fog began to unveil the pink predawn sunrise. Captain O'Neal rolled over, rubbed his eyes clean of the night's fitful sleep and gave Cyrus a nudge with his boot.

"Up with ya lad. Go relieve Jeb from night watch, will ya?"

At this first stir from the pirate camp, a chorus of blood curdling screams assaulted the campsite from all directions. The Timucua war party pounced as one, retribution fueling their rage.

The command, "To arms," had scarcely left Captain O'Neal's mouth when he was struck down, his skull split from crown to chin with a war ax. The others were tomahawked before ever gaining their feet. Jonesy was the last to die, mouth agape with eyes wide in panicked surprise, his headless last gasp lost upon the vapid fog.

The pirate's dreams of rescue, hidden treasure and the wealthy lives they would live, expired with them in a sandy pit behind the beach. No trace of them would ever be found.

At sunrise the Timucua paddled away on the outgoing tide and the ghost crabs got about their grisly work…

…Two hundred and forty years passed before fate intervened. The island suffered hurricanes and reconfiguring of island landscapes. Dunes were washed away, high ground shifted, and new creeks formed. Secrets once hidden were revealed anew…

Year 1914

In the mid-1860s, the Austro-Hungarian Federation was in disarray. Germans, Austrians, Magyars, Slavs, Serbs, and Hungarians competed for political dominance in the European Empire. An attempt to mollify competing interests with a dual system, separating the military component from civil administration, was falling apart. Many subgroups felt disenfranchised and in 1889 Crown Prince Rudolf committed suicide. His uncle and first in line to the throne, Karl Ludwig, abdicated the crown to his nephew, Franz Ferdinand.

Archduke Franz Ferdinand was known for his inclination toward a volcanic personality and absolutism. The trait empowered him to strive to re-establish a strong central government, thereby granting far reaching autonomy to all the nationalities of the empire. He reasoned this strategy would insure the survival of his family dynasty.

Not everyone was happy with the plan. During a parade on Sunday, June 28, 1914 in the Sarajevo capital of Bosnia, Gavrilo Princip, a young member of The Black Hand opposition group, shot Franz Ferdinand and his wife, Sophie, dead in their motor car... a shot heard around the world. The assassination precipitated Austria-Hungary's war against Serbia. The Central Powers (Germany and Austria-Hungary) declared war on countries allied with Serbia, which began World War 1.

Future

The coastal city of Beaufort, South Carolina, chartered in 1711, was named after Henry Somerset, Second Duke of Beaufort, and Great Britain. Beaufort was the second oldest major British settlement in Carolina, behind Charleston. Indian wars and constant threats of Spanish invasion from the south passed into history when, in 1733, the founding of the Georgia Colony provided a buffer zone from the early threats. Thereafter, Beaufort thrived as a major shipbuilding center, and exporter of rice and indigo to Europe.

The American Revolutionary War, which was fought to win freedom from British rule, left the City of Beaufort relatively unscathed. Most of the fighting was centered on the siege and occupation of Charleston. Following the war, Beaufort's fortunes improved. Her plantation economy experienced an unprecedented boom as the nation's largest exporter of Sea Island cotton, making Beaufort the wealthiest city in the country. It also boasted one of the largest slave populations in the new nation. Nearby Port Royal Sound became a gateway to much of early American history.

The American Civil War changed everything. Beaufort was occupied early in the war following an 1861 Union naval invasion of Port Royal Sound. Native islanders called the battle "The Big Gun Shoot" because the roar of the cannons from the waters surrounding the neighboring island of Hilton Head could be heard for miles. The plantation economy collapsed with the abolition of slavery. With no labor force with which to work the fields most of the wealthy antebellum families left Beaufort, never to return. Many of the plantations were broken up and parceled out to former slaves.

The next eighty years were tough years for Beaufort. The era of Reconstruction saw the erosion of white political power. Local resentments ran high. Penn School, on St. Helena Island, was established in 1862 to help former slaves "catch the learning". Integral to The Port Royal Experiment, Penn School was a national test case for bringing education to slaves. A former slave, and native son, Robert Smalls rose to become South Carolina's first African-American elected to Congress. Black Gullah communities on remote islands were pretty much left on their own.

Time

Time is an artifice of the human condition. We alone, among all the earth's creatures, saddle the pace of our lives with the abstract concept of time. Three score and ten (70) is the Bible's measure of a life well lived, a cherished goal for most, a full measure within which to cram all that we are, will be, and have been. Then, we go back to dust, and time moves on.

For some, there is another dimension in which time moves more slowly. The aging process seems stymied by a power unseen but tapped into by a practiced few. So, it was of the Haitian grandfather of a black woman, Elsie Fripp, housekeeper for a staid white family of nineteenth century Beaufort. The Saint Helena Island Gullah shaman, seventh son of a seventh son of a Haitian slave brought to Fripp Plantation in the mid-1800s, gathered the sacred herbs and signs, spoke the words and concocted a special "medicine root" that he rubbed onto the foreheads of the "Massah's" grandchild, and one of his own seed. He declared they would live long lives to bridge the cultural gap between black and white, good and evil, and the sins of their fathers: one selling blacks into slavery, one buying them.

Time had other plans however. Deception, and a falling out of childhood friends, locked both into an adversarial relationship that spanned the next eighty years, pitting the fates of a future island shaman, or root doctor, and a future "High Sheriff" against one another.

A new industry, mining phosphate from the local rivers and Sea Islands, gave a brief respite from economic malaise until it too was ruined by disaster. The market for phosphate was the production of fertilizer, and more notoriously, the makings for gunpowder to fuel European armies readying for the coming storms of war. A fleet of phosphate mining ships plied local waters employing hundreds of black miners to free dive the creek bottoms for phosphate nodules. More intense strip mining of low lying islands with steam shovels left great scars upon the land.

The Great Hurricane of 1893 wrecked the fleet of phosphate ships, killing two thousand civilians, mostly black islanders, and destroying much of the City of Beaufort. When Clara Barton and the fledgling Red Cross appealed for aid to the Sea Islands to then South Carolina governor, "Pitchfork" Ben Tillman, he asked, "How many white people were killed?" When told it was two or three, his response was, "Why bother." The fate of distant island black folk figured little in Tillman's political calculus.

A city-wide fire in 1907, accidentally set by some young boys smoking in a barn, finished the job. Much like the fabled Icarus of Greek legend, Beaufort's fortunes had flown too close to the sun. Her wings clipped by disaster, she became one of the poorest communities in the state.

By the early 1900's, Beaufort's only surviving industries were truck farming and commercial shrimping. The City of Beaufort and her surrounding sea islands became, literally, the economic backwater of the Lowcountry... the end of the road.

Decades later, an influx of development capital would marry the incomparable natural resources and beauty of the Sea Islands, kindling Beaufort's rebirth, making it a Southern Phoenix of sorts, to once again become one of the most prosperous counties in the state.

And so, it came to be that three disparate twists of fate contrived to weave the improbable story of a man swept up in life's great game of chance...

CHAPTER II:
Ireland

"Fearful finding, frightful hold,

Three-fold chests of dead men's souls.

Buried deep, forgotten long,

Yellow gleams its siren song,

Of Old Ben's secret, never told."

Ian Hugh Cory came into this world in the spring of 1898 in the rough and tumble outskirts of Dublin, Ireland. Born with one blue eye and one brown, the young towheaded Cory's "stars" hinted at some fateful, future day. His father, Hugh Cory, Sr., was an overbearing alcoholic who worked the peat mines. His arrival home each day, bathed in the working man's odour and the stench of cheap whiskey, heralded nightly rounds of verbal and physical abuse. They became products of a beaten man, numbly acquiescing to his place in the Irish caste system, dead in hope and soul, knowing he could do nothing about it.

Hugh's mother, Erin, was a strong, patient, loving mother. She worked as a seamstress, saving a few pennies each month from her paltry income to buy used books for her only surviving child. Barren after the loss of her stillborn daughter Shannon, she was determined that Hugh learn his letters to better his station in life. In that all too typical Irish neighborhood young Hugh Cory had, for five days a week since the age of 12, missed the morning sunrise. He was already half a mile deep in the coal mines on his half-day shift tending the pit ponies that hauled the coal carts to daylight.

The occasional deep rumbling in the ground would spit out fire, dust, and broken miners, hardening the boy to endure the unendurable. Hardest for young Cory was caring for the ponies injured in those accidents. The poor brutes were, to his mind, the purest of souls. They suffered their toils in silence and rejoiced with an unleashed exuberance when loosed into the fields. He envied their apparent indifference to the shallow squabbling of their masters.

In the afternoons Hugh attended a Catholic school. Unlike most of the poor Irish children, whose education and spiritual guidance was limited to a fated caste system, young Hugh Cory's took a different path. Sister Mary found a keen intellect and inquiring mind behind Hugh's mismatched brown and blue eyes. His quick mind digested every assignment in a single sitting, able to recite each lesson, text and verse with an almost photographic consistency. The child was different, worthy of Sister Mary's greatest efforts.

Private tutoring was a blessing to Hugh's mother, and a wasteful curse to his beetle-browed father. Hugh studied Latin and was encouraged to read history's great works, such as the meager budget of the church would allow.

After school, Hugh would become his other self and run the dark streets with his friends.

This dichotomy of great potential and tremendous waste frustrated Hugh's mother and left Sister Mary shaking her head in wonder that the Lord should put so much promise and pain into a single soul.

The Irish spring brought with it a seasonal relief from the mines. Fathers and sons put aside their coal picks and shovels for plows and potato sticks. Spring time was planting time. Every hamlet had its potato fields. Pit ponies plowed the furrows, while following behind women and children poked holes in the fresh turned earth and planted potato cuttings.

Young Hugh Cory played rugby on the neighborhood team, earning a reputation as a tough and relentless scrapper. Standing five feet and six inches tall, he was broad of shoulder with the kind of God-given knotted strength no fitness regime could ever produce. A curly mop of red hair framed an infectious smile and those always searching, two toned eyes. If there was mischief afoot in the neighborhood, one could be sure Hugh had a hand in it, his quick mind ever-alert for the chance to turn a lighthearted prank. Mid-game fist fights on the soccer field were the norm; he could hold his own with the best of them. Even so, his friends often taunted him about his extracurricular reading, as a "mamma's boy". Fearful of the hopeless reality of their own pre-cast station in life, they lashed out at Hugh for daring to break with the dreary drumbeat their lives would surely become.

Partially to better fit in with his peers and to rebuke their taunts, Hugh became a member of a local neighborhood gang, the Roundtop Knights. Not a murderous mob, but rather it was a tight-knit group of young men engaged in petty thefts and turf wars as their only means of belonging to something larger than themselves. Hugh took on the gang tattoo, a red dagger encircled by a green snake, the fabled snake supposedly driven from Ireland by St. Patrick, or so legend had it.

As a sixteen-year-old, Hugh found himself living two lives. At home, he dodged his father's drunken Gaelic rants, offering his body as moat and shield to his adoring mother. He read the books she bought for him, and actually enjoyed most of them in the safety of her nurturing care.

"Poetry is the wellspring of the enlightened mind," she used to say.

His two favorite fantasies, though, were Robert Louis Stevenson's *Treasure Island*, and stories of the Irish folk hero, Cu' Chulainn. Such imaginings could carry him far away from the dirty meanness of his otherwise invisible life. Alone in his bed at night, young Hugh's imagination would set sail aboard the pirate ship *Hispaniola* with cabin boy Jim Hawkins. Together they lived one swashbuckling adventure after another on Treasure Island, fighting pirates and searching for hidden gold. Other nights he would fight epic battles against overwhelming odds standing alongside the giant Irish warrior king, Cu' Chulainn. They would stand triumphant in the Druids' Hall of Heroes. Outside of his imaginary life of adventure was the gang and its cocooned hierarchy where he had earned the respect he would never get from his father. Fighting, drinking, and petty crime was Hugh's outside reality.

One night it all came crashing down. Hugh's gang got into a turf war brawl with another gang, the Low Bottom Kings. Usually trash talking, posturing, and the occasional fist fight satisfied the teenage bravado. But that night was different. The leader of the other gang, Donovan, picked out Hugh for a personal challenge. The winner would win the day for "his team". Better than dozens of busted heads, the "mano a mano" challenge was the ultimate arbitration in the Irish gangland code of honor.

Both gangs squared off facing each other, creating a circle around their champions. The lighter built Hugh, circling for advantage, moved in and out of swinging range of the larger Donovan, who stood his ground, turning always to face his smaller, quicker opponent. Donovan taunted him with gang slurs, "You marble-eyed bastard. I'm going to bust your Roundtop skull."

Feinting a right cross to the bigger man's head, Hugh sidestepped the counter punch, coming in low with a tremendous left hook to the man's gut. Donovan doubled over as his breath left him gagging. Hugh stepped in, grabbing the big man's hair with both hands to keep him from standing, and drove a right knee into his face. Donavan heaved over to the ground, his busted nose spraying blood in all directions. Blinded by his own blood, and struggling to gain his feet, Donovan reached deep inside for the strength to gather himself. His mates urging him to "Kill the puny bastard! He dirty tricked you! Kill him!"

The crowd roared its animal rage. Hugh well knew the rules of a street fight: get your man down and don't let him get up. Finish it; his advantage was speed. He knew he could never match the larger Donovan's

37

strength, if he got into a close grapple with him. Hugh circled in for a finishing blow to the ear of his opponent but did not see Donovan reach behind his back to pull a thick bladed Leatherman's knife. As Hugh wound up for the final blow, Donovan spun on his knees and lashed out at Hugh's midsection, the blade ripping his shirt across at his navel. It just missed disemboweling him by half an inch.

From a "man-to-man" challenge, this test of bragging rights had become a death match. Hugh went berserk. He stepped in behind the slashing blow, grabbed Donovan's knife wielding arm, and broke it at the elbow across his knee. Donovan's animal shriek following the crunching sound of splintering bone, quelled the crowd. Hugh picked up the knife from the shattered arm and with feral rage in his eyes, shoved it straight into the chest of his adversary. Full to the hilt, he drove knife and man to the ground in a final gesture of defiance. Flush with adrenalin, Hugh seemed eight feet tall within himself. He turned to the Low Bottom gang with a guttural snarl and dared any man to step forward.

There were no takers. Members of both gangs turned on their heels and scattered, leaving a crazed Hugh and bloody, dead Donovan alone in the street.

The bloodied young Hugh Cory staggered through the door to his house. Confessing all to his suddenly sober father and horrified mother, he waited for the arrival of the town constable. At the ensuing trial, witnesses from both gangs gave conflicting accounts of the fight. In the background of the looming conflagration that was World War I, the town Magistrate, unable to discern the truth of the matter, chose instead to offer seventeen-year-old Hugh a choice; a long prison term or immediate conscription into the British war machine, soon to be off to war against the Germans in the trenches of France.

CHAPTER III
"The Somme"

Mustered into the Royal Marines, Hugh Cory's first duty station was aboard one of Her Majesty's battle cruisers sent to Commonwealth holdings in the Caribbean. The HMS *Farragut* made week-long stopovers at Trinidad, Tobago, Barbados, the Bahamas, St. Lucia, St. Vincent, and Jamaica to promote Crown interests and enlistment for the war effort.

Talk of war seemed far removed to the young Irishman, newly landed in paradise. Shore duty was relaxed. "No black, dirty 'ole of a coal mine 'ere," Hugh Cory thought to himself. Only green palms waving from sugar white beaches to the myriad of seabirds soaring above deep blue seas. Local island women were gracious and welcoming in all manner of enticements. Cory drank his fill of their offerings. He was particularly drawn to the simple lifestyle contrasted to all his experience in Ireland: absolute freedom, simple, no worries.

To Cory, the entire island encounter was captured in the expressive, exaggerated faces carved into palm tree masks by local craftsmen. His practiced hands soon rendered several rudimentary pieces of his own. The outside world must surely have it all wrong. Who could want to fight in a place like this?

Reality answered with orders to begin loading the first of sixteen thousand recruits from the islands who would ultimately join the war effort. HMS *Farragut* was returning to England.

Under close scrutiny of the Boarding Master, sailors tossed everything not standard service issue. Most of the "recruits" owned very little anyway.

"All you lads, stow your gear and make ready to sail."

"You there, Seaman Cory, dump that island tripe. There's no place for it 'ere in Her Majesty's Navy."

Cory's palmetto face carving smiled its regrets from atop the receding heap.

After six months duty in paradise, notice was given that "Hell was open for business". Upon his return to England, First Mate Ian Hugh Cory was transferred to the army and dropped into insanity's great meat grinder of lives and souls, World War One.

In 1916, Lord Kitchener's British Expeditionary Force was made mostly of volunteers and conscripts from all over the British Isles and its colonies. Having lost most of the regular army in earlier battles of 1914 and 1915, this new army drew its ranks from local communities, such as the 1st Newfoundland Regiment, the Tyneside Irish Brigade of the 34th Division, and numerous divisions named for the towns from which these men came. At the Battle of the Somme, in the summer and fall of 1916, this British Army would bear the brunt of the action against the Germans as the French attempted to wrest control of Verdun from the occupying German army.

Infantryman Ian Hugh Cory, of the Tyneside Irish Brigade, shipped out to France with his new mates in the spring of 1916. Hard-lived from similar backgrounds, and hard trained into a close-knit fighting group, they shared the same sense of place and loyalty many had left behind in the Irish gangs of their hometowns. A group of sixteen were particularly close. They drilled together, ate together, and played soccer together in free time. Infantry all, they knew they had to watch each other's backs. None had yet to see combat. This tight bond was the glue that kept nerves in check as they moved up to the front lines in late June of 1916 to participate in the largest Allied campaign of the war.

For weeks after their arrival at the front lines, Cory and his mates were assigned to work crews digging and repairing trench works and revetments.

When the whistle for a water break interrupted the endless digging, a sweaty Cory, stripped to his waist and leaning on a muddy shovel, looked back over his shoulder and spat toward the retreating Sergeant Smythe.

"Lads, I'd love to show 'im what 'e can do with that goddamn whistle."

"Aye, I'm with you on that score, mate. If we dig any deeper we'll be fightin' the Chinese too."

The Tyneside boys in the ditch works shared a good laugh, quickly interrupted by Smythe's pressing whistle and order, "Back to work."

Clueless pawns to history's whims, Private Cory and his mates were mirrored by their German counterparts a quarter mile away, cursing their own Sergeant Smythe.

These opposing British and German networks of offensive and defensive trenches paralleled the Somme River, across the mid-section of France, for miles in each direction. They defined what was to become the bloodiest patch of ground in human history; "No man's land".

After months of endless preparations for the coming battle, Regimental Commander Jonathan Beaumont called his men to morning mess. Addressing them from a podium of ammunition crates, he chose his words carefully. He knew that uncertainty was the foot soldier's greatest enemy.

Hugh Cory and his mates gathered around.

"Men, tomorrow morning begins the action for which you have been training these last few months. As you know, our task here on the Somme is to blunt the German invasion of France, to kick their Hine arses back across the river and all the way back to Germany. It all starts here tomorrow."

A great wave of patriotism roared out to meet Beaumont's words.

"Tomorrow, July 1, 1916, is to be our greatest day. A morning barrage will clear the German defensive lines, after which each regiment, with its own battle plan, will take the field. If our artillery does its job, we should roll over the Hun defenses and begin the march to Berlin. All regimental commanders will have their troops called to by 07:30. Good luck and God bless. I will see you on the field, gentlemen."

At 5:30 the next morning, twelve thousand tons of shells, from fourteen hundred and fifty guns, rained down on German positions, turning the once pastoral countryside to the likeness of the dark side of the moon. The great yellow and orange streaks of powder and shot reaching skyward, the ground shaking so hard that a man could not hold his footing. Hell had truly come to earth. After two hours, nothing stood taller than a dead man's helmet to mark what had been there before.

The unanticipated consequence of British artillery rule, to not drop shells within three hundred yards of British troops for fear of hitting their own men, meant that most of the bombardment fell beyond the first line of German trenches. Supply and reserve trenches were heavily bunkered against such an attack. This strategic blunder left the German front lines almost entirely intact.

Sunrise behind the British front lines found Private Cory's group of sixteen friends taking morning mess together and attending a "make-do Mass" around an altar of mortar shell crates. They made small talk about "after" and swapped good luck charms and crude jokes to ease the pre-battle stress.

Cory mocked one of his mates from an anxious sense of false bravado. "If the Germans can't shoot any better than you do, Jimmy boy, we'll all be just fine." Turning to another, Cory added, "Alton, your skinny arse ain't worth a bullet."

One soldier passed a picture of his wife to Cory. "'Old on to this for me, just in case."

"C'mon, mate, 'old it yurself. We'll be drinking wine in Paris by the end of the week. Ern't no Germans could survive that bombardment."

Regimental Commander Jonathan Beaumont, working his way along the forming battle lines, interrupted the good-natured ribbing. "Ready up, boys."

Private Alton Dunbar turned to grab his rifle and rucksack, before puking out his last meal. With ashen face and trembling hands, he joined his mates marching toward the sound of the guns.

When the 7:30 orders to attack came, the British troops, who "topped the trenches" and marched into no man's land, suffered a withering hail of machine gun fire. Eight hundred and one men from the 1st Newfoundland Regiment marched into battle that day. Only sixty made it back unharmed. Five hundred of the eight hundred and one were killed outright.

Hugh Cory's Tyneside Irish Brigade of the 34th division started its advance nearly a mile from the German positions across open ground, in plain view of the German guns. A German flare was mistakenly assumed by Allied commanders to be a sign of early victory. German machine gun fire inflicted decimating losses on the advancing brigade, effectively erasing it as a fighting force with over one thousand one hundred casualties. Private Ian Hugh Cory returned alone across no man's land to the stunned British lines, all his sixteen mates lost, pawns to the great chess game of war.

Total allied losses on the first day of the Battle of the Somme exceeded sixty thousand men. Twenty percent of the entire British fighting force had been killed.

A German commander on the front lines opposing the British attack, was quoted as saying, "I forbid the voluntary evacuation of trenches. The will to stand firm must be impressed on every man in the army. The enemy should have to carve his way over heaps of corpses."

Thus, began a year-long battle of attrition, a standoff of constant shelling, infantry attacks and counter attacks that would define The Battle of The Somme.

Survivors of that first day, like Cory, were absorbed into tattered regiments to live the daily horror of trench warfare.

The front-line trenches, dug a little over head high, were winding, narrow and often flooded with muddy rain water. The zig zag design of the trenches was intended to protect masses of men from being killed by a single shell falling into the trench, the trench corners offering some lateral protection from gunfire and fragmentation. Some of the trenches had wooden batter boards for flooring to keep soldiers above the filth. Hastily dug trench works, dug at night to secure front line advancement from the prior day's battle, had no such luxury. Trench rats shared equal billet with the soldiers. Emboldened by the nightmarish conditions of the trenches, the rats aggressively invaded food stores, mess kits and waste piles, their unblinking black eyes missing nothing. They crawled equally among the living and the dead, squealing, squirming, and gnawing. Comatose, sleep-deprived soldiers lost ears, noses and fingers to the furry bunk mates. Constant shelling prevented proper care for the dead, whose heat swollen corpses bred disease in both armies. The smell, the stench, the entire experience was that of fighting a pointless, hopeless war in a sewer pit.

Shelling in no man's land often rained body parts into the trenches. The sulfurous thunder of the big guns loosened men's bowels; men went mad, and some jumped the trench alone, running to certain death to end the daily torture of fear and despair. And the chlorine gas, heavier than air, settled into trenches and fox holes to burn out the eyes and lungs of thousands of hapless soldiers who tore out their own throats and gouged out their own eyes in tortured writhing. German snipers routinely blew the brains out of anyone careless enough to risk a peek over the trench walls.

Unable to physically escape the endless nightmare, soldiers in Private Cory's squad sought that place within themselves that no German shell could pierce. Some wrote letters home to loved ones. One wrote poetry. Most all put unfounded faith in a lucky charm they would rub with a numb, metered cadence when hell closed in above them. Private Cory kept a copy of Treasure Island in his breast pocket for momentary escape from reality. All were more afraid to fail their mates than they were to die. When Cory's best surviving friend was killed by a sniper's bullet, he volunteered to cross "no man's land" at night to avenge his friend's death.

Cory's request was passed up the chain of command by squad leader First Sergeant Smythe.

Regimental Commander Jonathan Beaumont was in a tough spot. He suffered his men's agonies alongside them. He saw the senseless slaughter, the futility of sending hundreds of men to almost certain death in meaningless attacks to re-take a few yards of dirt. Six months into the battle had seen the front lines advance not so much as a mile, and at the cost of thousands. But he dared not speak of these things to his commanders. Orders were orders. He did have the latitude to authorize scouting parties and night time wire cutting operations. He was not opposed to the unconventional, if it got results and provided even a temporary lightning of his troops' spirits. Permission for Private Cory's plan to silence the sniper who was cowering the British lines was granted.

"First Sergeant, bring Private Cory to my quarters," ordered Beaumont. Fifteen minutes later, Beaumont addressed Cory, "Private Cory, are you sure you want to do this?

"Ey, sir. It's the wait'in that's killing me, sir. I'd much rather take it to the Hun than sit here waiting for the shell with my name on it."

47

"Well son, since it's your life in the balance, you pick your men."

"I already 'ave, sir."

They were two others from a Highland brigade, Tommy Wilkins, nick- named T-Tom because, at five feet two inches tall, he was shorter than his British Enfield rifle was long, and Neville Brownly. T-Tom was a light-hearted sort, always joking about, walking around on his hands like a jester, and looking at the bright side of things. He had a detached innocence that seemed to insulate him from the daily terror they all faced. Neville, though, was quiet and intense. He developed the stress relieving tick of fiddling with the safety on his rifle (click, click, click) to put his mind anywhere but in that trench. Country boys all, they had snuck through many a hedge-row in their youth to steal farmers' crops or poach a pheasant. The only difference between hedge-rows and barbed wire was the pheasants on the other side of the wire shot back.

Private Cory gathered his team on the front line. In a reflective moment they all shared a few pulls on Neville's tobacco pipe. Nodding to his mates and handing the pipe back to Neville, Cory rose and said, "T-Tom, Neville, let's up and away, lads." Neville cleared his pipe against a trench support and shoved it into his jacket pocket.

Off they went, as far out into "no man's land" as the forward-most observation trench allowed, only one hundred yards from the German lines and probable sniper's nest. Waiting for clouds to cover the moonlit battle field, they began a slow belly crawl, six inches at a time, so slow as to be practically motionless, inert clods scattered across the shell plowed ground. They eventually found a place in the German wire stretching across a shell hole offering just enough ground clearance for them to shimmy under without rattling the warning cans hanging in the wire.

There they could hear low, German voices beyond the darkness as they dropped into the German trenches. Cory was in the lead, stalking with the stone-cold courage of a man who had already known death up close and personal. T-Tom and Neville guarded their rear. The shadow of a man's head appeared ten feet around the next bend in the trench. He seemed to be a lone sentry, facing out to "no man's land" with his back to the trench. At a predetermined time, previously arranged with Commander Beaumont, British machine guns opened up across the trenches. At the first burst the German soldier grabbed his scoped, three-round Mauser 8 mm sniper rifle and stood up on a little wooden box to better his field of view of the certain advancing British soldiers. He never heard the subtle slither of a Sheffield trench knife unsheathed. *This would be easy pickings*, he thought, as Cory's razor-sharp commando knife silently slit his throat from ear to ear.

The Germans down the trench, opened up with their own machine guns, raking the night with green and white tracers. So loud was the gunfire echoing up and down the trenches that the gunners never heard or saw three strangers take out one machine gun, and the next, and the next, turning the German's guns on their own troops. The sniper's dead body had scarcely quit twitching, pumping its scarlet Arian blood onto raped French soil, before Cory and his fellows slipped back out of the German trenches, under the wire, and home, having silenced the sniper's nest and three machine guns-blood spilled atoning bloodied guilt.

Private Cory and his two buddies slept dry that night on clean bedding, following a hot meal and shower in the rear lines. All three would be medaled for extraordinary bravery in action...if they lived long enough.

The German trenches awoke to the fruits of the night's labors. That their best sniper and three-gun crews could be taken out in ghostly silence notched their haughty bravado down a few pegs. Who might it be the next night, or the next? Revenge was hell!

Cory's mind wandered in a moment of reflection. "I'm sent off to war as punishment for killin' a man who tried to kill me," he mumbled to himself. "But once here, I'm medaled for killin' a man who was trying to kill me. Go figure?"

The trio's relief was short lived. Twenty-four hours later Cory and his two trench rats were back to the front lines. For two weeks they fought from trench to trench, in the mud, blood, filth, and stench of the dead and dying on both sides. Life had no value, save the moment. Hugh's mood grew dark as he saw and experienced the mindless waste around him. Looking over at hollow eyed T-Tom and Neville, hunkered down in a muddy corner shivering, more from fear than cold, Cory thought to himself, *I'm a dead man walking. What difference do I make in this 'ole 'orible mess? Today, tomorrow, there's a German bullet out there with me name on it, to be sure. Reserve troops will be sent to stand their turn in this pointless grind.*

Mid-September of 1916 saw a push to break the German lines. More artillery barrages, more dead men hanging in the German wire. At three o'clock on a Wednesday afternoon a German gunner yanked the lanyard on his howitzer just as Cory was returning from the latrine trench. The shell landed in Cory's trench just beyond the corner he huddled against; in that last instant he realized that this one was close. The concussion burst his eardrums and hurled him to the ground. Stunned, he regained his wobbly legs and looked around the bend to check on his mates, T-Tom and Neville. He saw nothing of them except scraps of gut and cloth sprayed upon the trench walls. And inexplicably there, lying on the trench boards, was Neville's pipe, altogether unscathed. Cory numbly picked up his friend's pipe, turning it in his hand as if to comprehend what had just happened. It found its way into his breast pocket as reality slipped away.

Cory snapped. His mind unhinged, he leveled his rifle across the trench parapet and randomly emptied his weapon in the general direction of the German lines. Hit, miss, no matter, no purpose. The barrage stopped. Front line first officer, Sergeant Smythe, blew his whistle to form up and top the trench for the next open ground assault of the German lines. Private Cory stood wooden at attention, his empty rifle at parade rest, eyes unblinking, and ears numb to his commander's orders. Scrambling troops urged Cory to hustle up, but he refused to go. Not one more time would he top that trench wall. German gun fire raked the sand bags atop the trench. Screaming men were felled in mass, cut down by a scythe of machine gun bullets. A helmet, shot through the center, bounced back into the trench at Cory's feet, followed by its headless owner.

The blunted attack was over in ten minutes. Shattered stragglers fell back into their coffin-like trenches. First Sergeant Smythe slapped Private Cory across the face and back to reality, stepping astride the headless soldier at his feet to do so. "Coward, I'll have you shot!"

Cory was arrested and hustled away from the front lines. His mates watched his withdrawal like thirsty dogs begging for cold water, anything to get out of that hell hole.

Hauled before Commander Beaumont, Private Cory was asked to explain himself. In a shell-shocked stutter, he muttered a senseless limerick.

"To war we went,

Straight out from Kent,

Sixteen proud and true.

The Hun we met at River Meuse,

Save one, all lost, lament. "

Sergeant Smythe grabbed Cory, shaking him by the shoulders.

"The bounder's crazy. He should be shot for cowardice in the face of the enemy; executed in front of the troops to set an example."

Commander Beaumont knew Private Cory was no coward. He has already recommended he be medaled for taking out three German machine gun nests weeks earlier on a night raid into enemy trenches. Now, chained and stripped to the waist in the brig, Cory awaited his fate. Commander Beaumont noticed the gang tattoo on Cory's chest. It was similar to the one hidden beneath his own tunic, for he too had come from a hardened gang world in his British hometown of Bottlesworth. The hard scrabble lower classes often share a bond deeper than momentary conflicts. Beaumont's strength of character had enabled him to climb the "class wall" into a position of respect. Private Cory deserved no less.

"Sergeant Smythe, leave us a moment, and send for Corporal Bostwick from the rear supply lines."

"Sir? Smythe snapped to, with an insubordinate tone.

"Do as I say! Unshackle this man."

Private Cory stood numbly at attention, his catatonic stare focused on some faraway place, when Corporal Bostwick arrived.

"Corporal, I need you to do something for me, something off the record. Take this man off the field with this private dispatch and get him onboard the American medical ship at *LeHarve*. He has paid his full measure. And Corporal, please tell your father my debt to him is squared."

In "the fog of war", Private Ian Hugh Cory's transcripts were lost and he was subsequently listed as missing in action. Commander Beaumont knew he could not save most of his men from an almost certain fate. But for one, Private Cory, their shared bond of the hometown gang and his heroic action in battle were a ticket out of hell to a new beginning. By war's end, only two hundred of the three thousand men in four Irish brigades survived. Corporal Bostwick was safely one of them.

CHAPTER IV
To the End of the World

Thirty days after Private Ian Hugh Cory was spirited from the raging hell of the Somme, an American hospital ship carrying American war wounded and a few last minute allied strays stopped for re-coaling at Norfolk, Virginia. Those patients able to walk were allowed overnight shore leave. Cory, dressed in fresh navy blues and sporting a pocket full of cash won in a shipboard card game, settled in the nearest pub in search of that first taste of a cold American beer!

Hugh Cory's cockney accent was a big hit with the bar patrons. They all wanted to hear what it was like "over there": "Was it really as bad as the papers say? Are we winning? We heard you're some kind of hero, or something. What's it like to kill a man with a knife?"

As the drinks flowed into the night, Cory's demons began to stir. Today and yesterday traded places. His mind swirled with the haunting sounds of combat, of friends being cut down in waves of machine gun fire. The memory of the trench began to close in on him, and the sounds of the bar seemed a faded reality. When a drunken British sailor, whose amorous ambitions for a female patron herself hard-working Cory's cash wad, grabbed Hugh by the shoulder and shoved him to the floor, Hugh went berserk; it was gang thug Donovan attacking him again. It was the German sniper he faced in the trenches of France, and the reeling shock of being splattered with a friend's body parts that returned to his brain. *A weapon, any weapon!* A broken beer bottle appeared in Hugh's hand and he instinctively lashed out at the demons screaming from within. The sailor went down, blood drenching his mid-section. Others tried to close with Cory, to wrestle him to the floor, but none could hold him. His laughing cockney lilt became the savage roar of a man possessed. The bar cleared out, leaving him standing alone above the now motionless sailor.

The wail of sirens from fast closing military police blew the drunken cobwebs from Hugh's mind as suddenly as they had appeared. He knew the bloody sailor at his feet was a first-class ticket to the hangman's noose under British military law. He ran out the back door into a misty rainy night as fast and far as he could to get away from the war, the bar, and the demons haunting him. Private Hugh Cory of the Tyneside Irish Brigade closed the door on one life and leaped through the door of another.

Away from the wharves, away from the receding wail of police sirens, he ran toward the sound of train whistles in the distance. If he could hop a train to anywhere this night, he would be hundreds of miles away by daylight. His random choice was an empty supply train headed south for a return trip full of truck produce and food for the war effort. For two days Cory hid behind stacks of loading pallets in an open sided freight car. He was afraid to get off in a big town likely to have a telegraph and the law. His destination was the end of nowhere, wherever that would be; someplace where no one knew him or cared, someplace to hide and close off the world behind him. He jumped the train at a crossroads called Yemassee, South Carolina. Hiding behind some brush next to the tracks he watched crates of farm produce being loaded by black men from flatbed trucks onto train cars bound for northern markets.

The farm hands noticed the furtive peeking of a hunted man hiding in the shadows. They well knew the scenario, as many of them, at one time or another, had to hide from "The Man". When the produce truck was emptied, the white foreman moved on to the next car being loaded. One of the black men ambled over to a brushy corner, as if to relieve himself. Without giving any indication of another's presence, he called out in a low whisper, "Who dat be hidin' in de bresh? You be hidin' f'um de 'Man'? If'n you needs a place to hole up, you jes slip in the back o' dis truck, an we'll git way f'um 'ere. Lebdown en'tie 'e mout."

Cory struggled to understand the new tongue, but the man's hushed tone and head nod toward the truck conveyed all he needed to know. From the rail yard, Hugh rode in the back of the produce truck to Beaufort County and its Sea Islands. When the truck ground to a dusty halt beside a tomato field on the back side of Saint Helena Island, Infantryman Private Ian Hugh Cory of the Tyneside Irish Brigade had arrived literally at the end of the road to nowhere and into the spiritual sea island world of Gullah, "haints", root doctors, and Jim Crow.

CHAPTER V
Gullah 1917

Beaufort County, South Carolina, was a world in transition. Only fifty years removed from the Civil War, the county still bore the scars of the great conflict. Gone were the grand plantations of rice, indigo and Sea Island cotton. Gone were the financial windfalls of cheaper slave labor. Most of "The Masters" lost everything they owned to federal tax collectors and carpet baggers. The county's largest remaining asset was its rich farmlands. Truck farms, as they became known, were owned by black freedmen, a few locals who could buy back family land from the government, and wealthy outsiders. They produced corn, potatoes, beans, squash, lettuce, and tomatoes. The crops were still planted and harvested by black labor and trucked to the rail heads for shipment north.

Left largely to themselves, black communities on the islands worked the fields for paltry pay and kept up a small family farmstead for themselves. Former slaves, or Gullah, had their own social customs and beliefs that were a mix of white Christianity and African/West Indies culture. Gullah, a Creole blend of Elizabethan English and African languages, developed on the slave plantations in the coastal South. Outside was the white man's Jim Crow law, while inside the communities Gullah hoodoo doctors held sway on the islands. Island folk were close knit and protective of one another. They shared a common bond with anyone looking to escape white law, themselves having only recently shed the yolk of slavery.

The Fripp Community on St. Helena Island was a black community, named for the Fripp family that originally settled the land in the seventeenth century. Captain Johannes Fripp was a pirate buccaneer, awarded title to the land by the King of England for protecting British interests in the Carolinas against the Spanish and French. Fripp Plantation became one of the wealthiest plantations in the South Carolina Lowcountry, known for growing Sea Island cotton before the Civil War. After the war, many of the plantations' former slaves took Fripp as their last name. It was the home of Rufus Fripp that gave refuge to the run-away outcast Hugh Cory.

An upwardly modest home by island standards, Rufus' house squared thirty-feet by thirty-feet. Resting three-feet off the ground on pillars of red brick scavenged from the war ruins of the "Big House" on Fripp plantation. It was sided with overlapping white clabber boarding and topped with a rust-stained tin roof. A hand-railed front porch ran the full length of the house hosting several oak rocking chairs for casual gathering after a hard day's work in the fields. The house had one multi-purposed great room, kitchen, and beds for the children. There was one offset closed bedroom for Rufus and his wife Jezebel. The house had one island luxury, an indoor hand-operated pitcher water pump piped from a drilled well in the back yard. It fed the kitchen sink and a bathtub in the master bedroom. All other necessaries were tended to in the outhouse, placed well off to the side of the house.

Rufus' bible offered protection from all of life's known hazards, while the indigo blue paint covering the home's doors and windows guarded against the unknown spirits of Gullah legend, "haints", and evil spells.

Rufus' admonition to this new islander was prescient. It would frame the next forty years of Hugh Cory's life.

"Missa Cory, the onliest 'ting you hab to watch out fuh is runnin' foul wit de High Sheriff. He be comin' ober t'ere ebry now an 'gin, chasin' some fool dat gone an git he sef too uppity fuh de Man, or gots he sef drunk and kill somebody. Dat's when de High Sherriff he come. An' den you bes watch out. An speshly watch out fuh he dep'ty. He de deble own chile."

Rufus Fripp was a pillar of the Fripp Community. His family lived for six generations on the big island, first as slaves on Fripp Plantation, then after the Civil War as free men on their own small farm plots. Before the first bridges connected the islands with the mainland, none in his family had ever been more than ten miles from home. Rufus received a basic sixth grade equivalent education at the Penn School on the big island, the first such school to bring education to the islands after Emancipation. His family's last name, as was often the case, was adopted from the plantation his grandparents had worked on. Rufus may not have had much of a formal education, but he understood the entrepreneurial concept. By the time Rufus was thirty he had accumulated fifty acres of farmland.

Rufus Fripp served two masters: the Lord and his wife Jezebel. Where Jesus was ethereal and controller of the spiritual realm, Jezebel held a tight rein on all things earthen. Jezebel was named for the Jezebel in the Bible, an ancient warrior Queen of Israel. Rufus may have been king of his castle, but Jezebel ruled the roost.

"Rufus, warruh you tinkin 'bout bringing dis white man in my house? I done roll de bones and see nuttin' but trouble fo' dis man. He got de debil mark on em!" You heh de way he talk. Ain' no good come fum a man talk dat talk. An wheh dat I'lan he say he come fum?"

"Wife, dem bones de debil bones. De Lawd won' spite me fo hep a man in need. Trust in de Lawd."

Cory's limited experience with farming was digging potatoes back in Ireland. Still, farming is farming. Quick to pick up on his new surroundings, Cory soon became a skilled addition to Rufus' farming enterprise. On one harvest day Rufus and Cory were talking about how the white farmers could fix produce prices to their advantage, buying black farmers' crops, and reselling them at significantly higher prices.

"Whuh we gwine do Missa Cory. We's all hab small plots. How we gwine price up wit dem big fawms?"

"Rufus, we're going to organize an island farmers' co-op."

"Warruh?"

"That's when all your neighbors pull their crops together in bulk to compete with the big farms. You can compete, 'cause you don't 'ave the labor cost they 'ave. You are your own labor. This gives you a competitive advantage in pricing. You can demand top prices and take home larger profits."

Even though he worked hard to feed his seven children, Rufus Fripp still left time to serve as a deacon at the First African Baptist Church. Sunday mornings sitting on a back row was about as close to religion as Cory cared to get, given the total lack of any celestial benevolence he had experienced in the trenches of France.

It was the next Sunday service that Rufus brought the idea of the co-op to his congregation. To succeed in this novel plan, everyone in the Fripp community had to be involved. One crack in a unified front would jeopardize the entire effort.

Cory was ushered to the pulpit where he recited his plan, as he had to Rufus several days earlier.

"You'll all be knowin' the big farms are takin' the best of ya when they buy up all you can grow for a paltry sum, then add it to their own and double the price at market. Their price up is stealing what's your own. There is a way to make it right. It's called a co-operative. Seen it me'self in Ireland where the only competitive chance the small farms 'ave is to combine their efforts to work together to bring to market all they have, as one. All as one is the only way to get top price for your crops. You grow the same crops as the others, you should get the same price. It's the right thing to do for your families if the buyers won't be fair."

Big Sam, owner of one of the largest farms in the newly proposed co-op, stood to address the group.

"I yedde 'bout wha' you say. Maybe right be right, but right ain't always right. De Man, he ain' gwine like dis notion."

Rufus stepped up to Cory's side. "You right Big Sam, but less you wan' lay down t' de Man, d' onliest t'ing is fo' us t' stan' up, stan' up for Jesus. Let no man stan' alone but for the steady han' of the Lawd."

The congregation accolated a closing Amen.

A positive show of hands cemented the deal. The new co-op and talk of big ideas and bigger profits was the talk of the lunch social after church that day. Competing head to head with the larger white farms was new, and potentially dangerous territory.

News of a black farming co-op on the islands was also the hot topic of the next Monday morning breakfast meeting of a small, powerful group of businessmen in town. The largest stakeholders in Beaufort County's largest money-making cash cow, farming.

"It's the doin's of a newcomer out there at Fripp. My yard boy told me about how this new co-op was going to 'mesh up' with our properties."

"God damn niggers. Who do they think they are?"

"Sheriff, this can't stand. They'll eat into our profits, and times are hard enough as it is."

Big John, at the head of the table, slammed down a meaty fist and pointed to the sheriff. "You send Joe out there. Tell him to send those farmers a message. Not too heavy at first, but enough to get their attention."

All about the table nodded their heads in agreement.

"Next subject. Leroy tell us about the proposed new highway right-of-way bids. Who do we need to grease to lock this up?"

And so went the regular breakfast meeting of the town's Big Men.

With Rufus' support, Cory, white man and outsider that he was, became an accepted member of the Fripp community. Working together, the island's small farmers got better prices at the railhead for their produce than they could ever have gotten alone. This celebrity came at a price, however. One farmer's corn crop mysteriously caught fire late one night. Another's truck tires were slashed. And the second season's tomato and cucumber packing shed fees were suddenly increased by twenty five percent. The co-op's competitive edge, a continual thorn in the Big Men's sides, was lightly muted, but still they held on. Pride had no price!

Jezebel kept her silent vigil.

Newly accepted insider, but in a peripheral sort of way, Hugh Cory never really fit in anywhere. The only white face in any crowd, his two-toned blue and brown eyes were spoken of in quiet whispers lest "he lay he eye on you". His odd speech kept Cory in a figurative crowd of one, strangely like what happens to the black islander alone in a crowd of white people.

Cory helped Rufus work his crops, and those of his neighbors. He had always been handy with tools from his youth, a skill which he parleyed into the barter system of the islands. Little hard cash was needed for one's survival. One task of field work was worth a night's roof over his head, a warm bed and all he could eat.

Exhausted from a hard day's work, Cory sat on the tailgate of a pickup truck watching the sun set over freshly worked fields and wondered to himself.

"How is it these black women can work all day in the fields, carrying a newborn baby in a nursing sling on 'er chest and heavy loads of vegetables in a basket on 'er head with n'er a complaint? Me peat miners back 'ome in Ireland could learn a lesson or two from these folks."

The task system was a holdover from plantation slave days when the amount of work a slave could be expected to do in one day was called a task. Different jobs were measured in tasks. One task was the equivalent of working one quarter acre of land. Grinding twenty barrels of rice, picking so much cotton, splitting a cord of wood, were each measured by the task system. A slave could be told to work half a task in one field, and half a task doing something else. The small plot of beans, corn, peas, and squash behind Rufus Fripp's house could be hoed and raked in one task. Working a weeding hoe, rake, and a plow mule made for a long day.

Carpentry work kept Cory's clothes sewed and bought tobacco for his hand-rolled cigarettes. Whiskey was harder to come by. There was one honky-tonk bar on the island during Prohibition. It survived under the watchful eye of the High Sheriff and his cronies, who made sure they got a cut of any whiskey money on the islands as their "whiskey tax". Still, some of the island folk managed to hide a moonshine still or two from the law. Risky business, all the 'shiners knew avoiding the Sheriff's "Whiskey Tax" was one sure way to "git yo sef in trouble wit de Man". In island currency, a case quarter bought a pint of island "shine".

In between working friends' crops and the odd carpentry job, Cory would take a day to walk the wild beaches of Harbor Island. Harbor was a truly wild place with no people, no roads, and no houses. It was all palmetto scrub, wax myrtle, marsh cedar, and dense groves of live oak trees. But the beaches were glorious. To Cory, miles of wide open space, braced between an endless blue ocean, and sweeping dunes, was freedom. It was toes in the sand, and squadrons of pelicans gliding overhead on steady ocean breezes. It reminded him of his time in the Caribbean. Here, Cory's heart was free from his demons. His would be the only human footprints in the sand for weeks at a time, and he answered only to the rise and fall of the tides. Occasionally he had to outrun an angry wild boar, but it was better than German machine guns. Sometimes he would spend the night sleeping on the beach, staring up at the stars. Most nights were peaceful, but occasionally the past would come a haunting. The sound of surf breaking on the beach reminded him of the distant sound of cannon portending the 'morrow's battle. Old memories died hard.

Hugh Cory underwent a gradual metamorphosis, turning inward on himself, and shutting out more of the outside world. Future generations would diagnose this self-exile as Post Traumatic Stress Disorder, or PTSD. His increasingly odd self-talk amused and scared his Gullah friends. Hugh Cory slipped in and out of the spirit world. Walking and talking, he would address those physically present in front of him, and those invisible in *the other* world.

"T-Tom, Neville watch where you're walkin' mates. There's Huns about 'ere, don't ya know? You there, gemme back me mask. You can'o steal a man's face, can ya? If you steal a man's face ya, might as well take his soul too. There, there, Cu' Chulainn, warrior king me arse! Where were you on the Somme?"

On a cool October night Rufus and his friends gathered around for their customary fireside chat to share the weeks news, talk farming, and generally wind down with some "man time". Lengths of two by twelve lumber on cinder blocks circling a fire pit beneath a large oak tree at the head of a corn field next to a salt marsh creek was their council chamber. The crockery moonshine jug was freely passed around to lighten the mood and loosen the tongue. All of the Fripp community gossip was aired out around the campfire.

Rufus had just opined, "Dey's some tings bes lef usaid," when out in the darkness the men heard a rambling, disjointed soliloquy.

Talking to himself and gesticulating to unseen listeners, Cory walked into the circle of fire light, taking a seat as if late for the invitation. With Cory's arrival, a heavy cloak of salt marsh ethers, came drifting through the moss laden live oak trees, encircling the gathering in an effervescent glow. The mood around the fire became uneasy, the once cool, clear night air became heavy and damp in a blanket of fear. The men begin shifting on their bench seats, afraid to acknowledge what they all felt. Something gnawing, knowing, clawed inside their guts. One man, attempting to rise from his seat, was stilled by a haunting look from Cory's suffering eyes. Cory began a slow rhythmic Gaelic shuffle around the fire. His off colored blue and brown eyes cast wild looks around the muted crowd. Faster and faster he danced, throwing his head back and crying out to a blood red moon, which the men feared as being hell sent. He called out the names of his lost war buddies as if they were standing right there. He talked to them in his native Gaelic tongue, pointing to ghosts only he could see. The men around the fire sat frozen with fright. A final, tortured, primal wail of pain crumbled Cory to the ground, and for a long minute he lay there heaving. The fog of possession gradually lifted from his brain as he recovered himself. Looking around the campfire, Hugh Cory found he was all alone in the night. Across the yard, fearful eyes watched through parted blinds from windows painted in the familiar island indigo blue that kept spirits from entering portals and doors. Word that Cory was "touched" quickly spread across the island, and to the ear of the Gullah root man, Dr. Snake.

CHAPTER VI:
Dr. Snake

At daylight, two days after Cory's breakdown at the council fire, a very nervous Rufus Fripp shook Cory from a deep sleep.

"Wake up, Missa Cory. You gots t'git up. Doctor Snake ax fuh ya."

"Rufus, you're rattlin' me bones. What in 'eaven's name are you blathering about? The sun ain't even up good yet."

"It ent' de sun you hab t' be worryin 'bout Missa Cory. Doctor Snake done leabe you a sign."

Cory stumbled out of bed pulling up his shorts and rubbing the sleep from his eyes. He shuffled to the front door of Rufus Fripp's house, through the indigo painted portal and onto the railed porch. He was startled at the sight of a large, and very much alive, rattlesnake tied by its tail to the front porch railing. Around the snake's neck was tied a small hand-stitched red cloth packet about an inch square. The serpent's rattling buzz was an unmistakable warning of danger: "Don't mess with me."

Cory leaped five feet backwards at the rattler's strike, saying, "Holy mother of Christ, Rufus, what's this all about, mate? Some sort of prank?"

Visibly shaken by the unnoticed visit from a spirit man, Rufus replied, "No suh, Missa Cory. Dat a message frum Doctor Snake. 'E be wantuh p'laver wit you, and you bes be wantuh p'laver wit him, fuh I ent wantuh' him to put no root on dis here house."

"Who's Dr. Snake and what's he wantin' with me?"

"I spec 'E done yeddy 'bout yo sperrit talking t'odduh night. Doctor Snake iz a powful man. He hab de mo'rest strongest voodoo on de islands. 'E gots de black magic. Ent no body gwine mess wid Doctor Snake, 'cep maybe de High Sherriff. 'E kin pit de lub root on a man en he'll marri'd wid de mo'res oagly 'ooman in creeashun if she pay he price. 'E kin mek a man do mos anyting. Doctor Snake kin chew de root fuh you ifin you git in trouble wid the law. 'E kin make de judge let you go if he wantuh. En he kin put a conjuh on you dat you cain't wash off. Un time a field hand name Jerome done tek up wid 'nudder man wife. 'E beat ole Sam half t'def en shro 'em out 'e own house to lay wid dat 'ooman. Ole Sam gwine see Doctor Snake. 'E pay 'em ten-dollar tuh spell dat man an git 'e wife back. Wuh, Doctor Snake, 'E walk up dat house and knock on de door shree time wid dat walkin' stick o' his. He call out fuh Jerome tuh come out dat house! Jerome say he not gwine come out. He be peeking out de window when 'e see Doctor Snake chew 'e jawbone dis away an dat away. 'E wave a circle in duh sky wid dat walkin' stick, den 'e pint to duh ribber. 'E start talkin' in tongues, and den de mo'rest scariest ting happen. A blue head snake done stick 'e head out Doctor Snake mout and he call out tuh Jerome. Dat snake say, 'Jerome, you come out dat house.' En Jerome see dat blue head snake come out 'e mout, Jerome fall out to de flo'. Den Doctor Snake knock 'e stick on de do shree mo time an leave. Dat night Jerome wake up fum de flo and walk hesef down to de ribber wid out he say nuff'n. He walk scraight into de water an drown hesef. Dat who Doctor Snake is."

"What's that got to do with me?"

"Yo sperrit talkin' gots island folk wunnrin' if you gots de power too. Doctor Snake, 'e ain't gwine like dat notion. You gots to go see 'em."

"How do I find this Dr. Snake?"

"'E be watchin' out fuh you. You ent gots to find him, 'E find you. Dis night, you walk down to duh Chapel O' Ease 'bout sunclean fuh down. You take dis 'ere bell en ring it shree time when de sun go down, en wait a bit. 'E be deh d'rectly. You gots to git right wid Doctor Snake."

Jezebel stood cross armed on the front porch as she and Rufus watched Cory leave to meet Dr. Snake. "Rufus, you 'member what I say 'bout dem bones!"

70

The Chapel of Ease was built in 1746 as a place of worship for plantation owners who could not easily make the all-day trip to Beaufort, by wagon and boat, crossing twenty miles and two rivers. The chapel was constructed of tabby, a concrete-like building material made of fire charred oyster shells and mixed with water and lime. The mixture was then poured into boarded forms and dry cured, gradually building up the wall in layered sections. Door and window frames were likewise built into these formed walls. Wooden beams supported a roof system of hand split wooden shingles.

Spanish colonies in Cuba, Haiti, and Saint Augustine, Florida perfected the tabby building process and later exported it to the rest of the coastal United States with the slave trade. Paradoxically, it was the history of European exploitation of early Native Americans that made tabby construction so attractive for colonial America and the plantation system.

When early colonists settled the Sea Islands they found enormous mounds of oyster and clam shells arranged in circular patterns. The shell rings were often one hundred to one hundred fifty feet in diameter, with the circle's rings thirty feet in width and six to ten feet high. Almost always located adjacent to navigable water, these shell rings were later discovered to be abandoned Indian villages. Generations of natives lived atop the ever-growing piles of shells discarded from their steady diet of shell fish harvested from nearby waters and marshes.

Some shell rings have been proven to have been steadily occupied for hundreds of years at a time, over thousands of years of periodic occupations. The shell ring building period was carbon dated to have begun about 4,500 years ago, ending around 600 years ago. This archaic hunter/gather lifestyle died out with most of the native population after European contact. Foreign diseases, warfare, and greed finished off the native populations, leaving behind thousands of tons of ready building material for the newcomers.

Marauding British soldiers burned the Chapel of Ease during the American Revolution. It was rebuilt, only to be burned again after the Civil War. The history of The Chapel of Ease was as multi-layered as its tabby walls. Now standing as a burned-out shrine to history, the Chapel of Ease's only worshipping congregation is the worn and tilted grave stones of the forgotten dead. This was where Rufus Fripp sent Cory to meet Dr. Snake.

Chapel of Ease, July 2018, Courtesy Wollwerth Imagery
www.wollwerthimagery.com

Arriving at the appointed sunset, Cory entered the burned-out doorway of the chapel and waited for the last pink and orange salute of the setting sun before ringing his bell. Once, twice, three times he shook the bell. As the last ring faded into the gathering night, the hushed whisper of wings announced something had arrived. A hoot owl's eerie sermon floated on soft, dank breezes from a dark, roofless corner to the vines and creepers praying at the weathered marble alter.

Cory was a brave man, but even he started getting the creeps. A rising moon cast its soft glow upon the vaunted ruins. He waited five minutes, then ten, and turned to leave. Just as he muttered something about hoodoo foolishness, a twig snapped behind him. As he turned to the sound, he saw the outline of a man standing before the alter. He appeared to be a small man, thin with age, but firmly set. He was dressed in black with dark glasses and a straw hat. In his hand he held some type of stick or walking cane, but not as someone who needed it for support. This scepter had other purposes. It was made of a dark, spiraled wood, maybe wisteria, with a large knot at the grip, suggesting confident power and control.

A still moment passed between them, no words and no gestures. At the point the silence became awkward, Cory spoke, "Are you Dr. Snake? A friend asked me to meet you here. What do you want with me, and what was that snake on Rufus Fripp's house all about?"

The dark shaded man made no reply. Cory's attitude started to turn sour. He didn't go all the way out there to be trifled with.

"Listen up mate, Dr. Snake, or whoever you are. Rufus said I needed to meet you. 'Ere am I. If you have something to say to me, then let's be out with it. I don't know nothin' 'bout your island magic, I have me own demons aplenty to deal with. I'm not looking for any trouble with you." There was no fear in his voice.

The dark man stepped forward into a small patch of moonlight. In his right hand was the mysterious staff. In his left were two small cloth amulets measuring about an inch and a half square, one blue and one black. He said nothing, but with a deft motion of his staff, he drew a perfect line in the dust on the church floor. With his left he carefully handed Cory the blue amulet, then turned silently away and in three steps was engulfed by the darkness.

Cory stood in quiet thought, staring at the amulet. "This is mighty queer, it is," he said, and then he, too, turned and walked into the night.

When Cory returned to Rufus' house he was met by a dozen friends and neighbors. It was a brave man who meets Dr. Snake at night in the old church. That place is spook central to many island folks. Cory recalled the entire meeting with Dr. Snake to the crowd.

"What's with the line in the sand and the little blue bag?" he asked.

"You's a lucky man Mr. Cory. Dat black root bag was fuh if'n 'e 'tink you was gwine give im some trouble. Dat crossin' line say, 'Don' you mes wid me'. De blue root say he won' mes back wid you. Dat blue root fuh good luck, and t' keep yo demons away. Good gawd a'mercy, if'in 'e give you dat black root, you sho nuff be in a heap o trouble. You hap to move out o heh an take dat black root wid you, yes suh. You's OK now. You keep dat blue root close now, en don let it git wet. It lose it power if it git wet."

"Rufus, what's in the root bag that makes it so special?"

"Good luck fo' good, an' bad luck fo' bad. Doctor Snake pick 'em special to make de root. 'E put 'e speerit in 'em to give d' power. Could be dead man dirt fum de grave yard, 'o bird feather, maybe snake skin. Ain't safe talk um 'bout dees tings. Mr. Cory, I knows you say you come from a place call I'lan. I don' know nuttin' 'bout religion ober dey, but 'roun' 'ere, you got's t' be baptize in de name o' de Lawd. Next Sabboth we gwine take you down to de ribber an git you right with Gawd."

On the next Sunday, Cory, clothed in a full length white robe, was led down to a creek bank clearing to meet the entire congregation of the First African Baptist Church. The islanders knew Cory, inside, was kind of heart and gentle of soul.

"Don't you let nobody turn you 'roun'

Don't you let nobody turn you 'roun'

Keep the straight and narrow way.

I was at the river of Jordan

Baptism was egun

John baptized the multitude

But he sprinkled nary one.

The Baptis' they go by water

The Methodes' go by lan'

But when they get to heaven

They'll shake each other's han'.

You may be a good Baptis

An' a good Method' as well

But if you anin't the pure in heart
Yo' soul is boun' for hell."

After some "speech-a-fyin'" Rufus walked Cory waist deep into the slow-moving creek waters. With a joyous clapping and shouts of encouragement from the congregation, Cory was laid backwards and dunked to a series of "Amens." Rufus said, "Let de sin of de debil be wash away wid de tide."

The next few seasons came and went with more or less the same routine. Cory's occasional "fits" gradually became part of the island landscape. He hurt no one when "in de speerit". Though he was left conspicuously alone on these occasions, he was otherwise accepted as part of the island community. It was a sure bet no one was going to mess with him; he might have Dr. Snake 'put a root' on them. With no more tail tied rattle snakes and spooky meetings in the night, the general consensus amongst islanders was that Cory and Dr. Snake had agreed on a cordial, but mutually respectful, understanding.

CHAPTER VII
The High Sheriff

Cory occasionally rode Rufus' produce truck to the railhead in Yemassee to sell his crops. It was on one of these all-day trips that Cory first encountered the High Sheriff.

The High Sheriff, as he was called on the islands, was the vestigial representative of the white political power structure. His was the face of the law, "The Man". Black on black crime, usually in the form of domestic violence and petty theft, was largely ignored. Murder was an exception, as were crimes against whites, or their property interests, by blacks. The High Sheriff was empowered to use any means at his disposal in the performance of his duties. Few questions were asked by the authorities as to means, just outcomes.

The High Sheriff came to the department as a young man, serving as a deputy to his father, the elected county Sheriff. Small-town politics relied on mutual trust of the power structure to keep things as they were. Unexpected change brought the risk of "upsetting the apple cart". When the long-serving Sheriff died of a sudden heart attack, the Big Men in town fixed the election for a new sheriff, in favor of his son. Young in years but long experienced in keeping the status quo, the new sheriff stepped into his father's shoes as the High Sheriff. At six feet four inches tall, with a penetrating gaze behind dark green glasses and wearing a cross-holstered long barreled .32 caliber revolver, the new High Sheriff commanded unquestioned respect from even the roughest of island folks. The Sheriff could be fair when it suited him but was well known to be ruthless when crossed. Out on the islands, the law was what he said it was.

At the railhead another produce truck busted an overloaded axle and rolled sideways across the narrow two-lane road, blocking traffic both ways. It wasn't long before a patrol car arrived to straighten out the mess. The Sheriff, his deputy commander, and everyone at the railhead, worked to right the truck and push it to the side of the road.

The High Sheriff couldn't help but notice the only white face in the crowd. Pointing at Cory, he said, "You there. Who are you and what's your business here?"

Rufus Fripp took a big risk in speaking unbidden. "Missa Sheriff suh, dis 'ere's Missa Cory. I meet em on de rail while back en' giv'em a job workin' my place. He a good worker and don't cause no trouble, suh."

Cory fought hard to hold his tongue, thinking it better to play Rufus' hand, all the while looking the Sheriff straight in the eyes. Behind the Sheriff stood his deputy, slowly twirling his nightstick by a wrist thong, in an obvious display of intimidating, unchecked authority. The deputy's face was thick and expressionless. His cold black eyes unblinking behind reflective green sunglasses, a smoldering half smoked, half chewed stogie clenched between tobacco stained teeth. His stance resembled that of a bad dog on a short leash. Subconsciously Cory nicknamed him The Hun, after the jackboot Germans he fought in the War.

Offering a token of respect for his leadership on the islands, and knowing Rufus since he was a boy, the Sheriff asked, "Rufus, you vouch for this man?"

"Yes suh!"

"Well then, you men clean up this mess. You got trucks to unload."

When the Sheriff and his deputy drove off, all hands breathed a sigh of relief to have passed the moment without scratching the Sheriff's ire.

"Missa Cory, you gots t' be liddle 'round de High Sheriff. You bes off wid out he set 'e eye on you. Special watch out fuh he dep'ty. He nuttin' but mean white trash. He do all de Sheriff dirty work."

In the patrol car, the High Sheriff turned to his deputy. "I don't like the cut of that man's jib. Did you see those eyes? There's trouble in those eyes. You mark my word, there is trouble in those eyes! Keep a watch out for that one."

As the dust plume of the fast receding patrol car settled into the distance, Rufus asked, "Trip, you gots de relief wid you today?"

"Sho do Rufus. Gots it right under de seat'o my truck."

You bes' be gittin' it den. I 'tink dis be a good time to pass it 'round, 'cause I sho is relief de sheriff done gone from heh."

With that, Trip Legree pulled out a mason jar of his special island moonshine and passed it around. "Missa Cory, dis 'ere Trip Legree. He squeezin's set you right, an' I en't talkin' 'bout no scrap iron hooch neither."

Long accustomed to strong Irish whiskey, Cory confidently tipped the jug back. His eyes bugged out and he stumbled backwards with the first kick of Trip's island brew. "Whew! Good on ya, mate. That'll pop the knots out 'o y're string, to be sure."

The group laughed and collectively bid the sheriff good riddance and Amen.

Arial view of Harbor Island (top) and Hunting Island (bottom), South Carolina, and Atlantic coast (right) c. 1954. Courtesy Beaufort County GIS Department

CHAPTER VIII
Horseshoe Point

In 1925 Cory claimed squatters rights to a small spur of land thrusting out into the marsh at the end of the world, where the dirt cart trail dead ended at the inlet between Harbor Island and Hunting Island.

Access to the outside world was still by bateau, a thirty-minute pull from the north end of Harbor Island to the fish docks on St. Helena Island. It wouldn't be until 1939 that President Franklin D. Roosevelt's New Deal public works program built the swing-bridge and causeway connecting the two islands. It gave work to local laborers and sparked interest in the beauty of the barrier islands.

Cory got himself a "sometime" island woman named Masie. Masie was born half-black and half-white, the result of her single mother being raped by a white man. Masie was never fully accepted by the island community and was looked down upon as a reminder of the callous regard the whites had for blacks. An outcast herself, she had an immediate rapport with Cory. She cooked and sowed for him, nursed his aches and pains, and most importantly, understood his internal struggles. Masie was a calm harbor for Cory's stormy soul.

Such things didn't sit well with Rufus Fripp, though. Giving Cory no real room for argument, he solved the situation by announcing, "Missa Cory, we's gwine hab a weddin'."

Cory and Masie were married in the island tradition of "jumping the broom", but in a small white church on Seaside Road, with the Reverend Rufus Fripp presiding.

The tradition of "jumping the broom" descended from an old African Ghana ritual in which brooms were waived above the heads of newlyweds and their parents to sweep away old relationships and sweep in the new. The practice evolved in Southern American slave communities where formal marriage between slaves was prohibited by white slave owners.

A legally recognized marriage was held to be a civil contract, and as such, required the consent of free persons, something obviously running against the interests of slave owners. "Jumping the broom", while carrying no legal authority in the white man's world, was the Gullah declaration of a committed relationship. The tradition lasted on the islands long after emancipation. Rufus Fripp performed the ceremony and gave them each a "slave dime" to ward off bad spirits and bring good luck. The silver coins were pierced at the top edge with a red-hot nail and worn around the neck on a braided horse hair or cotton lanyard. The dimes were a reminder of "belonging to someone else" and were believed to protect the wearer from spirits.

"Masie, now you's a proper and marry up ooman by Gawd good grace. You bes' be tek care dis man. An' Missa Cory, you's right wid Gawd, marry a scrong ooman, an in good grace wid de chuch. Today a bless day."

Together, Cory and Masie built a mahogany driftwood shack from scrap dunnage lumber that washed up on the Harbor Island beaches. Cheap as American southern slash pine, the tough South American mahogany was rough cut for shipping containers bound for the United States, and later thrown overboard on the return voyage. Hard enough to bend nails, it also resisted termites.

Cory & Masie's shack on Harbor Island, late 1950s. Courtesy College of Charleston, South Carolina

The shack was a pretty basic affair, located just off the Harbor Island beach road in a grove of palmetto trees. A sixteen-foot by twenty-foot plywood floor system was laid over sawed-off palmetto tree stumps. Floor joists, wall studs and ceiling rafters were all built of mahogany. An open front room/kitchen and single bedroom comprised the layout. Amenities included an outside rain gutter and cistern to feed water to the kitchen sink, outside shower, and privy. Bathing was a sometimes thing, best taken advantage of when it rained.

An old lawn mower engine was mounted sideways on a stand between two saw horses, its grass cutting blade replaced with a circular saw blade. With this home-made table saw, Cory ripped heavy lumber into half-inch thick planking for simple overlapping siding. A mismatched assortment of doors and windows was scrounged from island friends, some painted indigo blue, others just plain, sun peeled white. Used tin roofing completed the job. A small front porch with driftwood handrails was added as an afterthought. Even brand new, Cory and Masie's house had a certain "island patina", suggesting to any passersby that the house had been there forever.

Cory called his squatted piece of land Horseshoe Point, for the annual springtime mating ritual of horseshoe crabs. The Point was about fifty yards wide and ran south across the salt marsh of the Harbor Island road for about two hundred yards, ending in a bluff overlooking a tidal creek. The horseshoe crabs migrated shoreward from the ocean by the thousands, in paired mating couples, insuring the survival of one of nature's most enigmatic creatures. They and Cory were spirit brothers, each with a rough history of survival. Cory descended from a line of Irishmen, surviving a thousand years of rule by outsiders: first the Romans, followed by Saxon raiders, and lastly a parasitic British Empire. His spirit brother horseshoe crab, closely related to spiders and scorpions, has been around for four hundred and fifty million years. Simple looking enough from the outside, the underside looks like something from another world. Two matched sets of three spider-like legs on each side of a hairy slit of a mouth, each with a pincer at the end. One pair of pushing rear legs and a smaller pair of feeder arms and pincers for carrying food to the mouth. They had long been exploited by a migratory bird, the Red Knot, which targets the annual spawning run of the crabs. Each female crab can lay sixty-thousand to one hundred twenty-thousand eggs. The Red Knots, on their annual spring migration from the southern tip of Argentina to the Canadian arctic, gathered in mass to feed upon the protein-rich buffet. Men, too, took a toll. Thousands were harvested to make commercial fish bait.

Fate can be a cruel mistress for both man and beast. For the horseshoe crab, it would be as a blood donor to future scientific researchers harvesting the crabs' blue copper rich blood to make anti-toxins. For Cory it would be to find himself, to find safe anchorage for his soul in the coming storm his life would become. Cory seemed to accept this brotherhood of outcasts, which he expressed in the horseshoe crab masks he made.

During the annual mating season there was no lack of horseshoe crabs perished in the effort. They rolled up on the beach or were marooned in the marshes. About a foot wide and two feet long from head to tail, the horseshoe crabs' shells were cleaned of legs and innards before drying in the sun.

Everybody for miles around could tell when Cory was drying a season's harvest of horseshoe crabs because of the awful stench of a hundred green shells curing on the racks out behind the "Point". The buzzards gathered atop a gnarly old pine tree, drawn by the stench. Cory carried about him a certain "s'attardant odour" for a week after harvest, no matter how much lye soap he used.

A light coat of varnish preserved the dried horseshoe crab shells. Most masks he made for tourists had island designs painted on them, from the rounded main body shell to the hard-bony tail. Some though, were specially made to order for Dr. Snake. He simply copied the hand-delivered image onto the masks. Some were animal reincarnations. Others were strange faces, with eyes painted over the bulging, brow point eyes of the crab. The three-dimensional relief made the faces come to life. He didn't know what they meant and he didn't ask the courier who took them away.

Palmetto carvings were altogether different though. Scattered about island beaches at the high tide line like pick-up-sticks, storm-felled palmetto trees offered an endless supply of material to Cory's practiced hands. Sawing them into two-foot sections, bark shaved clean and hollowed out, he revived memories of a better time and place into the staring faces pulled from the soft wood, each one a repository for long lost youth and innocence.

Besides working in the fields, Cory made his living from the river, catching crabs, oysters and clams, and bartering for fresh produce, tobacco and moonshine whiskey from Gullah farmers. Occasionally he worked a gill net with one of the island's more colorful characters, Trip Legree. When the tides were right and the local fish market prices were high, catching several hundred pounds of fish a night was worth the effort and risk. A three-hundred-foot-long gill net, with a three-inch mesh, was staked out across the entrance of a favorite creek. Cork floats kept the top line on the waters' surface, while a bottom lead weighted line kept the net tight to the floor of creek bed. Outgoing tides forced the fish from the smaller creeks to deeper water, and through the net. The three-inch holes, or mesh, allowed small fish to go through the net. Larger fish got caught by their gill flaps as they tried to squeeze through. The tasty and commercially valuable redfish was quick to sell at the fish docks with no questions asked. Game wardens, though, took a dim view of such large hauls. To the self-sufficient working man, creel limits were more of a suggestion than a hard and fast rule. One night, Cory and Trip had just pulled Trip's bateau up to the Island Seafood docks to unload their catch, when out stepped a game warden who had been watching them from the bridge with his binoculars. He confiscated the fish and impounded Trip's nets and boat, pending payment of a $500 fine for poaching and being two hundred fish over the limit.

Most law enforcement types would think they had burned Trip pretty good, teaching him a lesson that would keep him off the water for a while. The very next night the pair set an identical net in the same exact spot and caught enough fish to pay the fine and redeem Trip's boat and gear. And to top the night off to the good, they shrimped the outgoing tide with Trip on the oars and Cory throwing the net, catching a good fifty pounds in the sheen of St. Elmos's Fire. Each stroke of the oar and swishing cast of the net flashed a phosphorescent green on that dark black water, an ebbing green strobe adrift on the tides.

Most times, though, Cory and Masie stayed to themselves. He gigged redfish and flounder under the moonlight on the marsh flats off Horseshoe Point and fished for trout in the deep hole of the creek with bait minnows he trapped in the small salt water pond in the marsh flats nearby. He and Masie took long, lazy walks on the beach during high spring tides. He made up lilting poetry verses that she tried hard to understand, peering through the veil of the outward Cory into the man within.

"Cory, why you always reading from 'dem high tone books?"

"Masie, girl, you believe in the Bible?"

"Sho do. We's all got to get right with the Lawd."

"Well, girl, there's a larger truth out there than we get from the Bible and the folks in town."

"I don' know nothing 'bout that."

"Readin' the world eases me pains. There's places as beautiful and comforting as me native Ireland, and people as kind and gentle as you, sweet Masie."

On high tide moonlit nights, they poached the occasional sea turtle nest for an apron pocket of eggs. All the islanders knew turtle eggs were much richer than chicken eggs, and when in season, couldn't be bested for making the finest breads and cakes.

Some of the redfish Cory caught were so large, he had to nail their tales to a heavy board and scale them with a garden hoe. The large scales were the size of silver dollars. He used some of them as "make do" checker pieces. Fish fillets were grilled over an open fire, while oysters were steamed on an old piece of roofing tin. Blue crabs boiled in the pot, and rainwater barrels supplied drinking needs.

Each morning started with a fresh brewed pot of "settlers coffee" made from the dried and ground leaves of the naturally caffeinated local island shrub called Yaupon Holly. In stronger blends, earlier Indians drank this brew as a man's stomach purge, while holy men used it as a hallucinogen.

Life was pretty good for the AWOL, shell-shocked Ian Hugh Cory of the Tyneside Irish Brigade. He was happy living off the radar screen, even before there was such a thing.

Always handy with tools, Cory supplemented his meager lifestyle with carpentry work for local Gullah folk, and the slow trickle of white folk beginning to build beach houses on "his" island. In 1925, the State of South Carolina began paying Cory a small stipend to use a narrow access road across Horseshoe Point to service a supply barge for the lighthouse keeper on neighboring Hunting Island. One upside of island growth was that the local raccoon population used Cory's Horseshoe Point as a travel route from the wild salt marshes onto the island to rummage tourists' trash cans. Oak roasted raccoon was a regular in Cory's diet; a big boar 'coon was worth five dollars in island barter trade.

One night, after a shared meal of roasted oysters and fried redfish around Cory's Horseshoe Point camp fire, Cory asked his best friend, "Rufus, how do you cook your 'coon?"

"Well, Missa Cory, afin' you clean 'em up, you gots tuh cut out dem purple knot on 'e back an under 'e arms. If'n you miss dat, 'e stink de pot so bad, you jes well shro 'way de 'coon an eat de pot. Afa dem purple knot out, you par boil em 'till all de fat burn off. Den I cuts em up like chicken and fry em. En sometime I jes brown em in gravy and eats em on rice. Mos' taste like chicken too."

Irreparably shattered by the horrors of war, all Cory wanted out of life was to be left alone with his whiskey and tobacco. His was a conflicted soul, a mirrored host to mankind's sins and foibles. He carried the terrible burden of guilt for being the only survivor of his regiment. On starry nights he and his whiskey bottle would wobble through the marsh cedar trees out to the end of Horseshoe Point to fall asleep to the background song of surf rolling on the beach behind him and the myriad night life noises of the marsh.

Island folk gave him work when he needed it and friendship when he wanted it. Masie was always there for him, her soft brown eyes and gentle touch gave him shelter from his torments, nursing him through screaming, sweat-soaked nightmares. They often took moonlit walks on quiet beaches, returning with the rising sun. To his neighbors, he was accepted, like a crazy cousin who lived life on his own terms.

Horseshoe Point was known by other names and other people in earlier times. Pottery shards in the sand and along the creek bank were left by earlier Native American inhabitants from as long ago as four thousand years. They, too, recognized the Point as an easy access to the bounty of the salt marshes. If only the old, gray bones of the giant oak tree half buried in the creek bottom could talk about the sights and sounds passed beneath its massive crown in the last five hundred years, locked within the gnarled fibers as the sea slowly claimed its life.

By 1930, The Great Depression gripped the country. Its ripples were felt to the ends of the earth, even in faraway Beaufort County. Where money was the currency of life, people suffered when there was little of it moving about. Fortunes were lost, businesses failed. Those who couldn't adapt or accept, chose death by their own hand. But out on the islands, the financial storm had little effect on island life and its barter system. No stock market crash a thousand miles away could affect the exchange rate of a twenty pound 'coon for a pound of bacon, some flour, and salt.

Hugh Cory wanted nothing to do with money, or power, and all the pain that came with it. He spent his time making driftwood trinkets, horseshoe crab masks, and carved palmetto totems with images from Gullah tales.

Those he sold to tourists for paltry sums. Portuguese glass fish net floats, sea shell bracelets, and animal carvings made from driftwood, hung from every angle of his modest shack. He weaved strong, supple shrimp nets for local island fishermen, and for sale at Koth's Grocery in town.

Koth's, across from the courthouse, was the social compass of the town. Gossip was traded over fresh boiled peanuts, cold Schlitz beer, pickled eggs, and pickled pig's feet. Creaky, worn wooden heart pine floorboards registered every visitor's footfall to Old Man Koth's silent gaze and keen ears. Lawyers, doctors, laborers, and laymen made their appointed rounds to Koth's. Kids brought their Saturday collection of empty soda bottles for the two-cent bounty paid on each, trading them for Bazooka bubble gum, fireball candy, candy cigarettes and juice filled wax chewies. Icees and boiled peanuts were considered staple foods for teenagers on summer break. The huge ice locker out front ignored meddlesome FDA suggestions about mixing customer's wild game with the always-present aged half-beef hanging on steel hooks. Custom cut two-inch steaks, venison sausage, ban-sawed frozen drum fish, fresh shrimp, and crushed or block ice, all passed through this magic porthole. Beer, ice, gas, bait, gun shells, beanie weenies, and advice, whether you needed it or not, all proffered at Koth's. A single gas pump by the road fed local sportsmen's weekend adventures.

Cory made the twenty-mile hike into town twice monthly. His jaunty stride suggested he had an urgent appointment somewhere. Dressed in cut off kaki britches and tire rubber homemade sandals, t-shirt or bare-chested, his friendly nod of tobacco-stained beard and tasseled white hair to passersby was a familiar sight to most locals. The library lent him copies of Homer, Milton, Edgar Rice Burroughs, and Steinbeck to feed a thirst his mother imparted to him those many years ago in Ireland. On some of his trips into town Cory had to suffer a routine shakedown from the Hun. The Hun did it just because he knew Cory was not afraid of him, never realizing that such banal harassment made the small man big and the big man small. Some folks saw Cory as a slightly crazed old man, some as an eccentric Irish hermit.

Local folks, recognizing in him the wildness and absolute freedom from the shackled lifestyles they lived, envied his carefree indifference to the hurries of their world. His was a lifestyle that rose and ebbed with the ocean's tides, as natural as each daybreak leaves gifts upon the beach. He came to be called Driftwood... Driftwood Cory.

CHAPTER IX
Fearful Finding

In town, the world was not so simple. Times were tough. Even the Big Men in town, those self-anointed few who controlled the banks, the courthouse, the law, and most of the land, were feeling the pinch of the Great Depression.

One cool, fall morning, the now-monikered Driftwood was making for the creek bed off Horseshoe Point. He dropped off the high bluff into the great swath of golden Spartina grass that reached out to a blue-sky horizon, interrupted only by the lazy meandering of creeks and dotted marsh hammocks. He was headed for a bed of large, single select oysters he knew were accessible only when a west wind blew the tide extra low for a few critical hours. A five-gallon bucket of single select oysters was worth a pint of rum or half a week's groceries. The water was clear and cold, but shallow enough not to top his heavily patched black rubber boots. He shuffled along casting his eyes about the shelly bottom for the silted outline of palm sized single oysters. Being in the low tide creek bottom sheltered Driftwood from the raw wind above. He wore his ratty canvas jacket rolled and tied around his waist, and his faded pink long johns rolled up to his elbows. The curls of blue smoke, rising from the pipe he recovered from Neville's body at the Battle of Somme, were but a nervous distraction for the Great Blue Heron hunting his breakfast of mullet and fiddler crabs. When Driftwood turned the last bend in the creek at his favorite oyster bank, he found it already occupied. Two large raccoons were fighting over a freshly-opened clam and didn't see him until he was close enough to give one the toe of his boot.

"Bugger off, or you'll find yourself me dinner guest this evening."

Driftwood set to work with his picking hammer and oyster bucket. It was hard work digging the succulent shellfish from this particular oyster rake, because it had grown in and around the bones of a giant oak that once grew upon Horseshoe Point. One of many hurricanes over the last few hundred years had undercut the high bank with the tidal surge that made these storms so dangerous, toppling the giant into the deep tidal pool below the bluff.

Working slowly along with his hammer, Driftwood noticed the unnatural square end of a piece of sawn lumber jutting out of the muddy bank. It was studded with old, hand forged spikes. His carpenter's interest piqued, Driftwood dug further. The still ebbing tide washed away his diggings revealing more timbers, and something else. It had a rounded surface strapped with metal bands. "What 'ave we here, mates," he mused.

The next hammer blow punched through the worm-eaten wooden shell and shiny gold coins, a double handful of them, spilled into his hands and into the mud. Driftwood hastily filled his pockets from the cascade of gold, while looking quickly around to make sure no one had seen him. No one knew where he picked his oysters, so the secret was safe. No one could ever know. Once revealed, the secret would drag him back to the world he fought so hard to escape.

Knowing he couldn't possibly excavate all of the gold in one tide, he plugged the hole with a chunk of salt-hardened oak and hurried to high ground. Back in his shack, Driftwood carefully withdrew the muddy coins from his pockets and washed them off in a bucket of rain water.

"Masie, come quick, girl. Look here what your man found in the creek."

The irregular round coins were all crisply stamped, not minted like modern coins. Of roughly equal size, they all shone with the luster of freshly struck gold. Spanish doubloons! Clearly visible were the mintmarks and initialed monogram of the Spanish assayer who made them: a king's ransom dancing in the hands of a pauper.

"Nary a word now to anyone about this. Do you understand me, girl? This 'ere is trouble to be sure."

"Lawd, Lawd 'usband. If'n de High Sheriff fine out 'bout dis, 'e be on us like white on rice. You bes turn loose dat gold. Dat dead man money."

Driftwood was careful not to draw unwanted attention as he went about his daily routine. He worked every other low tide for the next six months, hauling his weight in gold coin each time, plus a bucket of oysters to keep up appearances. The original treasure chest had become three. Three thousand pounds of coin he pulled from beneath the old oak tree, one thousand pounds from each chest. Each trip he sang a little ditty, and smiled, thinking of what the rest of the world would do with such wealth.

"Fearful finding, frightful hold,

Three-fold chests of dead men's souls.

Buried deep, forgotten long,

Yellow gleams its siren song,

Of Old Driftwood's secret, never told."

Wars have been fought over such treasure. Driftwood knew the destructive power of gold. Having shed himself of both war and money, he decided to rebury the gold on a remote palmetto hammock, half a mile south of his Horseshoe Point. Inspired by the marooned pirate Ben Gun in his worn copy of Treasure Island, Driftwood buried it under the roots of a large salt water cedar tree, lining the hole with a canvas tarp, and building a hand sized trap door under a foot of soil.

"Never can tell when I might need a little shiny salvation me' self," he thought, whistling a little tune as he worked.

While the Great Depression didn't hurt Driftwood's self-sufficient lifestyle, Prohibition was putting a crimp in his evening libations. As was normal for small towns at the time, most anything worth owning belonged to a privileged few. The High Sheriff and his cronies controlled the only bars and speak easies, conspicuously open in spite of whiskey laws. This included the black honky-tonk at Club Bridge Creek on St. Helena Island. A creek side general store by day, Club

Bridge was a favorite island watering hole by night. Recent raids had closed down island stills. With his normal supplier shut down, Driftwood had to use his meager cash savings for the store-bought whiskey that kept his demons at bay.

Former Club Bridge Creek general store, July 2018
Courtesy Wollwerth Imagery www.wollwerthimagery.com

Walking ten miles sober to Club Bridge was easy. The return trip, loaded up on island hooch, was another thing altogether. Driftwood's answer to this dilemma was his personal "tide taxi". He would row his skiff the more or less five-mile straight line to Club Bridge Creek on an incoming tide. He'd drink until he passed out or ran out of money. Then, with help from other patrons, he would clamber back into his bateau, and sleep it off. The outgoing tide would carry him back toward Horseshoe Point where he would wake up to the morning sunshine and within sight of home.

The Club Bridge area was home to two businesses, three if you counted the country store turned honky-tonk by night. Club Bridge itself was a modern macadam road bed paved over the original wooden bridge structure. The under pinning was oyster bed and barnacle encrusted creosote pilings. On the seaward side of the bridge was the Maggioni Oyster Canning factory, with its own barnacled loading dock, and inward, the Club Bridge country store. The store, too, had a creek side dock running the length of the store. But this dock had one special adaptation. Beneath the grocery store sales counter, liquor bar by night, was a trap door to a hidden storeroom beneath the floor. It was to this room illegal whiskey was spirited by boat at night, unseen from patrons, the road, and prying eyes.

Few but Driftwood fully appreciated the uncanny marriage of his two favorite pastimes Club Bridge presented; unlimited booze topside and fantastic Sheepshead fishing below.

Roadside, the Club Bridge store had a single gasoline pump, ice machine, and assorted advertisements posted on the sunburned pine clabber siding on the front of the building, the largest being a faded Standard Oil sign.

When the Standard Oil sign was seen tilted off-center, that was the sign the bar was open for business. To those unknowing, the juke box in the back corner, framed by two pool tables, was but an oddity for a simple country store.

One Saturday night Driftwood was full of rum, and short on funds to pay for it. Threatened with a thumping or jail time if he couldn't pay up, he dug into the lining of his jacket and plunked down a shiny gold coin.

"How's that fit your pistol, bucko?" he said, with a twinkling of his one blue eye.

The bartender, who owed his life to the company store, and the Big Men who owned it, quickly pocketed

99

the coin and shoved a full bottle of rum into Driftwood's hands while hustling him out the back door.

"It's on the house."

At 9:00 the next morning five businessmen were sitting around a breakfast table in downtown Beaufort, where they routinely met to discuss their mutual affairs.

The Big Banker was protecting one of the group's constituents. "You say that black boy wants a loan to open a wholesale carpet store? How's that gonna 'fect Bill's stepson's business?"

"Based on his financials he's gonna cut your boy's ass. He don't need that big profit margin to feed his family."

"Well, then, stick it to him. If he can pay double rates, let him ride. If not, that'll shut him down or I'll pay for lying."

The Sheriff threw his pet project on the table. "Boys, this new highway 21 extension can be a big win for us if we can get frontage access. We need to get our surveyor buddy plugged in for a percentage, carve off some access frontage from the surveys on the sly and we can control development along the main corridor to town. They'll never see it coming."

"And what about you, John? You been eyeing that new golf course on the island. How we gonna make any money on that sand pit? That out of town developer has already squared the deal."

"Leave that to me. The head clerk at the permit office has a boy with polio. I've made sure his boy gets the medical treatment he needs. He's on board." Nodding to the Big Banker, he continued, "I know things about that other bank. His financing package is dependent on those permits and we got that aced. No sewage plan, no permits, simple as that. We'll buy it for a song, wait sixty days and re-apply for our permits. No worries, I got it wired."

A knock on the back door to the power room stopped the discussion. It opened to the face of a sweaty bartender who placed a shiny gold coin on the table, maybe the answer to all the Big Men's money problems.

They grilled the bartender, passing around the gold coin as they peppered the nervous man with questions about how that coin came to the bar.

"Who is this Driftwood Cory, and where would he get this kind of money?"

The High Sheriff inquired of the bartender. "Does this man Cory have one blue eye and one brown eye? Works odd jobs out on the island?"

"Yes, sir, Sheriff, that's him. It's hard to tell which eye to look at when I'm talking to him. That's the man though, kind of spooky. He comes around the bar a couple times a month, but I ain't never seen him with no gold before."

"Damn it. I knew he was trouble the first time I saw him. He was working for old Rufus Fripp back then. The Limey bastard stared me straight in the eyes. There's no back down in that man. He and his half breed wife live in a shack at the end of the road on Harbor Island, selling driftwood trash to tourists."

"Well, Sheriff, what are we gonna do 'bout it?" asked one of the Big Men. "The man spends most of his time in the river. He could have found a single coin on the beach. It's happened before."

"Yeah, well, I don't believe in coincidences. Look at this coin. It's in mint shape; never been circulated. No damn way he found this on the beach. Boys, we all have land money, but damn little hard cash. We can put on a good show for a while, but if this depression doesn't ease up soon, all of us could go under."

The Big Banker added, "Hell, my bank is playing a shell game with nervous depositors' money as it is. One big run on deposits and I'm done. All y'alls paper is in my bank, too, so that means when I have to call your notes, you go down with me. We're all done."

"Sheriff, what do you propose we do about this Driftwood fella?" asked another at the table.

Knowing there was slim legal cause to "talk" to Driftwood, the sheriff saw an opportunity to exercise his disdain for those who didn't fear him. Besides, his chief deputy could use a good workout. "I'll find an excuse to haul him in and see if we can sweat some information out of him. Do you realize what raw, untraceable gold could do to solve all our problems? If that son-of-a-bitchin' mick is holding out on us, I'll beat it out of him. Who's gonna miss a man like that anyway?"

CHAPTER X
Sensible Dirty

You have basic, cooked in a steel drum, stump hole moonshine, that'll wreck your innards and rot your brain. Then there was that lovin' potion teased from a mixture of island grown sweet corn, wild rice, and sugar cane syrup, all fermented to perfection and cooked in a proper copper still. It was run through charred oak whiskey barrels for that, so hard to describe, but infinitely satisfying, tongue tingling sensation that was "Trip Legree's Squeez'n's". "En't no finer drinkin' liquor on the islands," he often boasted.

"Trip" Legree got his nickname from his crippled right knee, crushed as a child beneath a stumbling plow mule. The bad leg and hobbling gait proved no disabling infirmity. At over six feet in height he looked over most island folk, his furtive dark eyes saw everything. His soft, hyphenated speech was quick and to the point. Forearms like banded steel did the work his bad leg could not; pulling oars and fish nets with the ablest of men.

Trip didn't have the luxury of a lengthy childhood. His father drowned while night shrimping when Trip was ten years old. He had to grow up fast, working the fields and river to help his mama feed the family. He never had the opportunity to attend the Penn School, so he never learned to read. "Di'nt need no schooling to read the ribber," he proclaimed. Like Driftwood, Trip worked a little bit of everything to get by. His real calling came one night while sitting around the campfire with the elders, "listening to Gullah tales of the old times in Africa, the hard times before 'mancipation', and the risky bidness of making moonshine whiskey," as he put it.

By the time Trip was twenty years old he had earned a reputation as the best "shiner" on the islands. It was a dubious title though, inviting trouble from "The Man". With prohibition in full swing, and hard caught blue crabs bringing only ten cent a pound, the lure of getting $40 a gallon for moonshine, proved irresistible.

Running liquor was a sketchy business. You had to have the whiskey sold before you make it, so you don't have the evidence hanging around for too long. One had to have a desolate spot to set up the still, hard enough for the sheriff's deputies to find, but easy enough to get in and out with the bulky raw material needed for the job. Trip's copper still could make 30 gallons of liquor per night. Secrecy was paramount: never make a batch the same time of day, the same days a week. It' was best to work at night to hide the smoke from the still's fire, and on windless nights, too; the smell of raw whiskey makin's, adrift on night breezes, was a sure give away.

On a cool fall afternoon, Cory was out back of Horseshoe Point, trout fishing, when Trip rowed up in his bateau. "I got's some bidness t' talk wid you 'bout, Missa Cory. You knows I makes a little whiskey now en' agin. Well, my fireman done gwine en gots his sef sick. I cyan run de still by my sef. If'n you hep me dis night, dey's a free gallon in it fuh you. All you gots t' do is keep de fire burnin' while I do the makins'. You meet me down to de corn field back Ole Sam house sunclean fuh down.

Driftwood, never one to shy away from a little work, or a chance to acquire a gallon of fine sippin' whiskey, agreed with a nod of his head. "An' don' let nobody see you," added Trip.

The night's work went as smooth as Trip's island shine on a Saturday night. By daybreak they had just about finished loading 30 gallons of whiskey into the back of Trip's truck when they heard the buzz of a low flying plane overhead.

"Quick, out dat smoke."

Too late. A loose tongue had tipped the sheriff's men that Trip was making up a batch of "shine" that night, and they were on patrol. Both men worked swiftly, trapped on a dead-end dirt road, waiting for the wale of sirens and baying trail dogs. With nowhere to run, they waited nearly twenty minutes, but still no "Buckruh". They eased the old pickup to the edge of the field and looked up and down the road for the law they knew had to be hiding there. The road was clear.

"Saints be praised. Haul ass, mate!"

The sheriff's information had been accurate. The deputies knew where the still was hidden. They knew Trip and Driftwood were cooking whiskey, but still they held off. It wouldn't be until two weeks later that they busted Trip's still. They caught him with 60 gallons of whiskey and $2,400 cash money.

The budget for local law enforcement and the sheriff's salary was largely paid with fines collected from whiskey runners, illegal bars, and prostitution. Corruption was rampant, and openly condoned by local custom. Law enforcement, and those making a living on the fringes of society, played the same game. Both needed each other to survive. With no fines there would be no operating treasury. Without corrupt law there could be no profitable crime to make illegal money to pay the fines.

Whiskey raids, like the one on Trip's still that night, gave the sheriff something to put in the local papers about his crime fighting successes. "A whiskey ring was broken up, the perpetrators fined and given 60 days on the chain gang," was the front-page news story.

The raid had been delayed two weeks after finding the still so Trip could make enough money to pay his fines, pad the sheriff's wallet, and have enough hidden away to rebuild his still for another day. It all made good, absurdly normal business sense. The sheriff kept the whiskey, some for his friends and deputies; the rest was rebottled and sold in the bars and speak easies controlled by the sheriff and the Big Men.

Trip proclaimed, "Dat sheriff dirty, 'e sensible dirty, though."

CHAPTER XI
Frightful Hold

Out at the Fripp community, everyone on the street scurried for cover like spooked fiddler crabs, when the High Sheriff's car came cruising slowly by.

"En't no good gwine come from dis when de High Sheriff be lookin' 'roun," proclaimed one of the elders.

The High Sheriff's 428 police interceptor came to a crunching stop on the gravel rock road beside a group of island folk. He rolled down the window of his patrol car, exhaled a blue ring of cigarette smoke into their cowering faces and lowered his dark sun shades.

"Any of you people seen Driftwood?"

"Nawsuh, Mr. Sherriff, we en't see'm."

The Sheriff's stiff stare said he knew they were lying, and they knew he knew. Using his middle right finger for emphasis, he pushed his sun shades over his eyes and drove on toward Harbor Island.

Driftwood and Masie were out front of their Harbor Island shack, mending a local shrimper's net, when the Sheriff's car came sliding to a halt in a cloud of dust.

"Masie, girl, you'd best be goin' inside now. Slip out the back door. Run and hide down by the creek bank. It's me he's wantin'."

The High Sheriff got right to it. "Driftwood Cory, I'm arresting you on a charge of making bootleg whiskey with Trip Legree. You and I are goin' to have a little chat down to the jailhouse." With handcuffs in one hand he eased back his jacket flap to expose the grip of his long-barreled .32 revolver, suggesting it was non-negotiable.

By 5:00 that afternoon Driftwood Cory was in the Beaufort County jail.

A Sheriff's deputy hauled Driftwood inconspicuously through the back door of the jailhouse, past the day prisoners' cells, and down into its bowels to a small isolation room with a cell door. It measured eight feet by eight feet, with no windows, and a low ceiling. It was Spartan, dank, and dark, with a single mattress in the corner and a hole in the floor for the latrine. The smell of stale urine hung heavy in the air. A single light bulb dangled from an electric cord just beyond the gray rusted cell door. Near the stairwell was a small wooden table and two chairs.

Meanwhile, the outside world went about its daily business, ignorant of the drama unfolding beneath its feet. Another sunrise and sunset passed.

Driftwood had no way to tell how long he had been in the cell. One hour, one day? It was all the same dim, dank, monotonous sameness. Only his internal body clock told him it was way past supper time, maybe breakfast time too. He was powerfully thirsty. Like a caged dog, resigned to an unknowing fate, he lay down on the filthy mattress and willed away the time. His mind wandered to the beach on Harbor Island, walking barefoot in the surf. He dreamed he and Masie were behind their shack heading a mess of shrimp for dinner. His mind was anywhere but in the tiny, dark room below the street.

Late into what had to be the second night in jail, Driftwood stirred to the noisy blaring of a radio from somewhere above, repeating the same song over and over again, a dozen times or more.

Extreme, prolonged isolation from sunshine and the normal interactions of daily life can play tricks on the mind, outing itself in delusions and altered realities.

"I must be losin' me grip," Driftwood thought. "And what in 'ells nature is that damned racket?" He hollered to the darkness, to the grimy walls of his prison, and the oversized cockroaches, busily tending their business about the filthy floor.

Ev'ry mornin' at the mine you could see him arrive

He stood six foot six and weighed two forty five

Kinda broad at the shoulder and narrow at the hip

And everybody knew, ya didn't give no lip to Big John

Big John, Big John

Big Bad John

"Who dat down deh in dat hole hollerin' out de ground?"

The voice seemed to come through the cast iron sewer pipe from above the cell.

"I's Juble. Gots all tangle up wid ole scrap las' night, took drunk and heh I is. Who you?"

Driftwood called back to the voice in the pipes. "The sheriff pinched me for makin' liquor with Trip Legree. Got a bulge on for me I canna' fathom."

"You dat Cory what work wif Rufus Fripp?"

Big John, Big John, Big Bad John

"What's wrong with that damn radio?"

"Ain't nuttin' wrong wit dat radio, Missa Cory. Dat de Big Boss Man run dis town. He and 'e friends own mos' ebryting round eh, 'cludin' de radio station."

Somebody said he came from New Orleans

Where he got in a fight over a Cajun Queen

And a crashin' blow from a huge right hand

*Sent a Louisiana fellow to the Promised
Land, Big John*

"When Missa John an' 'e friends git a mad on an'
gather up a 'drinkin', 'e call up de radio station an tell 'em
play dat song till 'e tell em stop. Sometime it play all night
till day clean next. When you hehs dat song play all night
ebry body know dey's a bad day a comin' fo somebody.
Dat dey fightin' song, dey white man hoodoo.

Big John, Big Bad John

It was near daylight the next morning on the
outside when footsteps came creaking down old wooden
stairs. The rheostat for the single light bulb was cranked
up, and the lightened face on the other side of the bars was
that of the High Sheriff.

Another man sat darkly shaded in the stairwell,
marked only by the soft ember glow and the wafting
stench of tobacco. The Sheriff pulled the table and a chair
from the corner of the room and sat in front of the cell
door, plunking a glass jug of ice water on top of the table.
Cool rivulets of condensation sweat off the jug and
dribbled tauntingly across the table onto the floor.
Driftwood could feel his throat tighten at the sight of such
wasted relief, only inches beyond his grasp.

"So, your name is Cory, the one they call
'Driftwood' out on the islands?"

Driftwood said nothing.

"I knew you were trouble the first time I saw you
with Ole Rufus Fripp that day in Yemassee. I run things
in this town, and that means men like you have to know

111

their place. Stare me in the eyes, will you? You got to show respect for your betters. You can stay down here and rot for all I care. Nobody knows where you are, and most wouldn't give a damn. I had you arrested on a bootlegging charge. I can hold you long as I want, or until you tell me what I want to know."

The Sheriff popped the top off the water jug and took a long, deep swig. Try as he would, Driftwood couldn't take his eyes off that water jug. His pride compelled him to steely silence.

After a few moments he asked, "What do you want with me, Sheriff? I keeps to meself, me and Masie. We 'aven't broken any law that I know of. You didn't catch me runnin' whiskey."

"You got a secret, Driftwood. You found yourself a little stash of gold somewhere and you're going to tell me where it is. The bartender at the Island Club gave me this gold coin you used to pay your bar tab."

The Sheriff reached into his shirt pocket and pulled out the coin, deftly snapping it into a spin on top of the table. The dull glow of Inca gold spun out from the light of the single overhead bulb, washing the walls of the grimy room in waves of gold avarice.

"I found that coin on the beach. You see how I live, just makin' ends meet fishin' the river and carvin' keepsakes for tourists. You think I would be living that way if I had that kind'a money?"

"Tell you what I'm going to do. I'm going to leave you to have a little chat with my deputy. We'll start over tomorrow. Maybe another day down here will improve your memory."

With that, the Sheriff rose and disappeared up the stairs with a nod to the man in the dark corner. Out of the shadow stepped The Hun, tickling the cell bars with his night stick as he unlocked and stepped through the door. A wicked, sadistic smile creased his heavy features as he poured the cold water onto the floor. Driftwood reeled in all conscious thought as the blows rained down. No one on the street above could hear the muffled grunts and thuds down in the Sheriff's "discussion room".

After a long while, the feeling started to creep back into Driftwood's arms and legs. His face swollen, hands bloody and skinned from fending off the blows. He crawled over to the mattress in the corner and sat upright, pulling his knees to his chest. His ribs hurt to breath. Driftwood had never been an overly religious man. The Somme took from him what little faith he had. He reached beneath his shirt and felt for the blue amulet and slave dime around his neck, rubbing them between his fingers while a dull sleep overtook him. When he awakened, there was a cup of water and slice of bread beside him.

Charlie, the black trustee jailhouse cook, sent out a message by the Gullah grapevine that "de High Sheriff done gots Driftwood lock up 'neath de jailhouse in dat hole." A sobered up Juble got all of Fripp Community buzzing, "What to do 'bout Missa Cory?"

Another chunk of timeless waiting and wondering came and went in the hole below the city streets. When Driftwood heard footsteps on the stairs he hid the water cup under the mattress and prepared for another beating. The Sheriff and the Hun stepped into the dim light.

"So, how are we feeling this morning? Sleep well? I did a little homework while you were entertaining my deputy. Seems like there is an outstanding warrant for an Ian Hugh Cory, something about a knifing in Virginia. Killed a British sailor, they say. Identifying features are one blue and one brown eye. That's a hanging offence in

Britain, isn't it? Tell you what I'm going to do. I have to try you on the whiskey charge, as a matter of court record. Then I'll have you sent back to England to hang. How's that fit YOUR pistol, Mister Smart Ass? That is, unless you've had a change of mind about that little secret of yours."

Driftwood did a lot of thinking in "the hole". A man can inure himself against repeated beatings, but he gets only one chance at a hanging. Why did they think he had more gold? Why would they resort to kidnapping and torture, if they weren't desperate? Then it hit him like an epiphany. *The Depression! The Sheriff and his cronies ran the town, but they were cash broke, too. No twenty pound 'coon and a bottle of rum could fix the money problems they faced*, he thought.

"Sheriff, you can't beat anythin' out o' me that did no' die back in the trenches of France a long time ago. You go ahead and have your trial."

"Deputy, talk to him some more."

"Give it up, cousin. You can tell me. Hell, we're family," the Hun sneered. "Who do you think is Masie's papa?"

Driftwood's hobbled charge was met with a wicked lead black-jack blow to the side of his head. Deep below the streets the leather covered black-jack did its dull work on a senseless body, while Driftwood's soul walked the cool beach of Harbor Island to the calming rhythm of the rolling surf.

Back on the island, a wizened old man, dressed in black, a straw hat, and dark sunglasses cocked his head, as if listening to a whispered, far away plea.

The Sheriff stormed from the jail cell, frustrated as all hell that he couldn't break a little man with the queer eyes and funny accent. He called a meeting with the other Big Men.

"Damn it. If I let Joe beat him to death, we get no gold. A whiskey conviction is good for a couple of weeks in jail and still no gold. If I have him hung, no gold. Son-of-a-bitch!"

Three days later Driftwood Cory was hauled into the sunlight, cleaned up, and given back his freshly washed cloths. The trial was on.

It was supposed to be a closed-door affair, a procedural motion with an automatic, predetermined outcome: a bootlegging trial, straight and simple. The players were all there. Judge Brown sat behind a large mahogany bench. The court stenographer sat to the right, the High Sheriff and The Hun stood at the handrail before the bench. Several quick fines and misdemeanor rulings on petty cases had already been dispensed. A meek handful of citizens sat in the audience.

How the word got out about the trial date was a mystery to the Sheriff. To his angst, there sat in the back of the courtroom old Rufus Fripp, Driftwood's wife Masie, and a dozen locals from the islands. In the middle of the room sat a man in a straw hat and dark glasses, the High Sheriff's long-time adversary, Dr. Snake. In his pocket jingled two gold coins, by way of Masie.

Masie and Driftwood's friends had all come to town in Rufus' farm truck. Dr. Snake simply showed up.

The judge gaveled the room to order. "Sheriff, you may present your case of the County of Beaufort vs Mr. Cory, of Harbor Island, on the charge of bootlegging."

"Your Honor. Mr. Cory," pointing to the defendant box, "is charged with running illegal whiskey. He has no permanent address of residence. He is a public

115

nuisance with no obvious means of support. Just look at him. Tattered clothes, unruly hair, and those wild, crazy eyes. I'm not sure the man's all there. The sheriff's office recommends jail time of ninety days to be served on chain gang, in lieu of paying a fine of five hundred dollars, and demolition of the squatter shack the defendant has illegally constructed on Harbor Island."

The sheriff turned his back to the empty jury box and gave a little wink to the judge. The fix was in. Surely Driftwood would come up with some gold, the key to finding the hoped-for hoard to get the Big Men out of their mess, and to pay a fine he had no other way to pay.

"Mr. Cory, have you anything to say for yourself before I announce my ruling?"

Driftwood rose from his chair and turned to the courtroom crowd. His arms spread in the manner of a pleading defense councilor, he began reciting the opening lines of Homer's "*Illiad*", in Latin (English translation):

> "*Sing, goddess, the anger of Peleus' son Achilleus and its devastation, which put pains thousand-fold upon the Achaians, hurled in their multitudes to the house of Hades strong souls of heroes, but gave their bodies to be the delicate feasting of dogs, of all birds, and the will of Zeus was accomplished since that time when first there stood in division of conflict Atreus' son the lord of men and brilliant Achilleus...*"

A stunned courtroom crowd, cast looks all around mumbling disbelief of what they just heard. The sheriff, mouth half agape and dribbling tobacco spittle, turned to the judge.

"What the hell was that?"

Masie turned to Dr. Snake sitting quietly, his eyes closed, his head and torso in a steady rocking motion.

"Order, order in the court!" shouted the judge, pounding his gavel to quiet the crowd. He leaned forward from his leather-bound throne, adjusting his spectacles to better see the newly lettered defendant.

"In plain English Mister Cory, if you please."

"Judge, I been a'livin' on the island since 1918, first with Rufus Fripp, and then buildin' me own place on Harbor Island in 1925. I'm no barrister, but I do know how to read. The book at your courthouse says my livin' there unchallenged for ten years grants me quit claim title to that little piece of land nobody was a'wantin' anyway. The State pays me ten dollars a month to dock the Hunting Island barge at my place. They wouldna' pay me if they thought I didna' own the land. I fish the river to feed me and Masie, and I make souvenirs for tourists. The Sheriff's charge is a personal vendetta against me. He can't prove I had anythin' to do with making whiskey. I like meself a wee dram or two every now and again, but there's no law agin drinkin that I'm aware of. His deputy over there should be in this seat instead o' me. You don't think I'd be a'gettin' these bruises beatin' meself up, do you?"

"Be careful, Mister Cory." The judge cast a quick questioning glance toward the Sheriff. He began to say something, then stopped mid-sentence, with an odd stuttering look on his face, as if he forgot what he was about to say. He locked eyes with Doctor Snake.

The judge turned to a surprised deputy. "Well deputy? Mister Cory is insinuating that you roughed him up. Is it your normal practice to beat up the subject of a misdemeanor charge?"

117

The Hun turned a leaden stare toward the Sheriff, who injected, "Your Honor, I can assure this court that my staff did not abuse this defendant."

"I want to hear it from the deputy."

The High Sheriff's face began to flush. Things were getting out of hand. His eyes said it all.

"Well, deputy?" prodded the judge.

"Your Honor, I nev—" His voice trailed off, his sentence unfinished. He began again. "I did not. Ah, well, your Honor, I might have been a little rough interviewing the defendant."

"And just where did this interview take place?"

"Ah, ah," he stammered again, trying to tame the words fighting to escape his mouth.

"*De hole, de hole, de hole,*" came into the deputy's ears.

"De hole, your Honor. We, I mean, I interviewed him in the holding room."

The judge surveyed the courtroom. All eyes were riveted, awaiting his next move. He couldn't shake the stare of the old man in the straw hat and dark shades mouthing something unintelligible. He was briefly mesmerized by the writhing of something inside his jacket?

"Sheriff, this defendant has grounds to prove quit claim title to his plot of land. He has proven means of support, and the support of his community. It is clear to me that your deputy's treatment of him while in custody was excessive. As the defendant was not caught making whiskey, nor was he caught in the possession of illegal whiskey, the charge of bootleggin' against him is dismissed. Mister Cory, you are free to go."

The High Sheriff was left standing alone in the courtroom, seething at the humiliation. "There must be another way to shake that sumbitch from MY gold."

CHAPTER XII
Chewin'd' Root

After the trial, Driftwood, Masie, and all their friends from the islands piled back into Rufus' truck to find a paper stuck under the wiper. He opened it casually, then bolted fully upright in the seat. He slowly turned to Driftwood, holding the note out by the tips of his fingers, as if it might bite him.

"It fuh' you. It fum Doctor Snake."

Driftwood took the note and read it quietly to himself, slowly forming the words with his lips, as if to more fully grasp their meaning. The letter ended, not with a written signature, but with the squiggly facsimile of a snake. No one made a sound. After a long minute, Masie had to ask. "Cory, what it say?"

120

"Well, girl, I've been invited to chew the root with Doctor Snake. He says the coins spoke to him; that the spirit world has a message for me. What coins is he talking about?"

"I pay Doctor Snake two yo' special coin tuh sit at yo' trial t'day. 'E was rubbin' em 'tween 'e fingers and hexin' when de judge and de dep'ty was talkin'. 'E say dem coins talk back to 'em, too."

Rufus draped his right arm over the seat, turned to Driftwood and looked him straight in the eyes. "Missa Cory, ifin' you goes to dat chewin' wid Doctor Snake, you bes unerstan' you's goin' whey no white man eber been afo'. En't no tellin' whey dat root take you."

"Let's go home, Rufus."

The following evening Rufus and Masie dropped Driftwood off at the old cart path leading to the Chapel of Ease. The note said Driftwood was to meet Dr. Snake there at sunset. They were instructed to come back for him "when de rooster crows" the next morning.

Driftwood was not surprised to see Dr. Snake appear from behind the marble pulpit just as the sun was setting. This time was different. Instead of lines drawn in the sand and passing of amulets, he was greeted with, "Come, please, sit down." *Was this the same taciturn apparition of their first meeting?* he wondered. "Mister Cory, I been watchin' you since you come to de islands, an outcast from yo' own people. En I seen de good in yo heart de way you treat Masie, en help Rufus, en de others. My sperit see you in dat hole 'neath de jailhouse an de evil dat after you. In de courtroom d'other day, dem coin Masie give talk'um me. Dey tell me a story 'bout blood money an' misery. De spirit world see all dese 'tings, Mister Cory. Dey's lot o good in dis world, and lots o' bad too. De spirit world tell me de difference 'tween what be what when I opens my soul talk'um me. You gots to open yo' soul t'hear what dey gots to tell you now. Will you let me show you de way?"

"I ain't scared o' no man, Doctor Snake. I got me own share of ghosts I'm livin' with, so I guess talkin' to yours won't hurt me none."

Dr. Snake began the ceremony, building a small fire in the well-used pit at their feet, donning a horseshoe crab mask of Driftwood's own making, commissioned by Dr. Snake many months before. Contrasting lines of black on white, exaggerations of contorted pain, snaked across the mask's face and formed a boundary invoking the battle of light and dark, of good versus evil. Fierce eyes glowed from shadowed slits where the crab's eyes had been. Knotted horse hair tassels like cat-o-nine tails lashed from side to side with his rhythmic movements.

The sounds of the night receded into the shadows, away from the growing firelight bouncing off the tabby ruins of the old church. Dr. Snake made sweeping gestures with his arms and uttered mysterious incantations to the spirit world, imploring them to come forth. He took a pinch of dried herbs from a small leather pouch hung about his waist, offered them to Driftwood with the motion to chew them, then took a pinch for himself.

The crunchy bits in Driftwood's mouth tasted at first like the bitter hulls of fresh cracked pecans, drawing the spit from his mouth like tincture of green persimmon. He was about to spit it out when a sharp tingling sensation exploded on his tongue, then traveled deep into his brain as a flash of light. Dr. Snake's words ran together in a meaningless babble, streaming from somewhere outside the both of them, channeling lost souls through the ghoulish grin of the mask. Dr. Snake threw something into the fire that flashed with a bright smoky effervescence.

The words became clear, but distant. Driftwood's eyes could see between the betweens, between the here and some other reality. Time became timeless. He talked to the ghosts of long dead pirates locked in Hell for the brutal price they paid for stolen gold, for the slaughtered Incas who mined it, for the innocents killed by evil greed to protect it. They begged Driftwood to release them to eternal rest by putting the gold to good use. These lost spirits vanished in Dr. Snake's smoky concoction, and in their place came the faces and names of almost 3,000 of Cory's mates from the 34th Tyneside Irish Brigade, all perished for the false pride of failed nation states.

A gentle rain bid, "Wake up, Cory, day clean nex' mornin'". All that remained of the night before were a few smoky wisps from the dying embers beside him. There was no trace of Dr. Snake, only Driftwood's haunting memories of the night before. Whether dream, nightmare, or a real trip into another dimension, Driftwood awoke with new resolve. He knew what he must do with his hidden treasure.

Driftwood had but just shaken to his feet when he heard Masie calling out to him from up the road. He walked out into the new day with a plan.

CHAPTER XIII
Three-Fold Chests of Dead Men's Souls

The Big Men met for drinks the evening after the trial.

"Sheriff, you can't break that man. Offer him a deal. We bury the hanging offence in England, in return for the gold."

"Hell, Sheriff, we don't know if there IS any gold. You may have beaten the shit out of an innocent man for nothing."

"Innocent, my ass. Nobody would take a beating like that for nothing. He's got it. Got it hid somewhere nobody will find it."

"Shit, Sheriff, there's a lot of 'nowhere' out there to hide it. Make the man an offer. Show us a couple coins to prove he has it. We'll swap the noose for the gold."

"Judge, I thought that was the plan in court the other day, to force him to show us something. What's the matter with you? We had him boxed in a corner and you let him off. You let that ole conjurer get inside your head, didn't you?"

"We'll just have to find another way, that's all," the judge said.

The next day a tan sedan delivered a sealed envelope to Driftwood's front door. After a quick glance, he asked the driver to pick him up the next morning at 7:00 for a ride back to town. He agreed to a meeting. Because they came to him, Driftwood instinctively knew he had leverage over the Big Men.

When he entered the John Cross Tavern he was ushered through closed doors to a back room. It was a room of power, with heavy, leather trimmed furniture, a bar, and a round table around which sat The High Sheriff, the Judge, the Banker, the City Attorney, and the Mayor. Mr. John had his own leathered throne. The Hun guarded the door. Heavy cigar smoke filled the air and several half empty shot glasses suggested a heated discussion. Most men, when summoned to the room, enter with hat in hand, as if asking for permission to even breathe the same air as the Big Men. Such was their sway over the town.

Driftwood though, walked in straight and tall, with a little confident swagger that unsettled even the Sheriff. There was no small talk, nor any civil greetings.

The Sheriff began, "This is how it's going to work. I have the proof I need to extradite you to England to hang. We'll sweep that under the rug in return for the gold we know you're hidin'."

125

"You canna' threaten me with 'angin'. Hell, I'm already dead, killed a thousand times with each of me mates at the Battle of the Somme. I got nothing left to lose. But you, who think you got a God-given right to run my life and everyone else on the islands, got a real problem. Behind all that cigar smoke and big talk, you're this close to losin' everythin' to the depression." He held up two fingers pinched only an inch apart to make his point. "You're leveraged up to your arses in debt with no way out. It's not you who have leverage o'er me. Tis the other way 'round."

"And the gold?"

"Aye, I got gold, three blinkin' chests of it. Pirate gold, doubloons, I think they're called. More money than all you bastards ever dreamed of. I've no use for money. All the money in the world can't bring back me mates and the livin' I've lost to war and the likes o' you. Since the gold standard was abolished, nobody can spend that gold in public. Won't do you no good if you can't find a way to spend it."

The Banker squirmed like he'd peed his pants. He shuffled to the side of Big John's throne chair and cupping his mouth to the man's ear, and whispered, "The market value of gold, at thirty-five dollars an ounce, pales in comparison to the historic value of mint fresh doubloons. This man is sitting on millions of dollars! That's many times the budget for the whole damn county."

Big John gave his flunky the nod to speak openly.

"I have contacts who can launder the gold through collectors and overseas gold exchanges."

Two smoke rings rose from Big John's stogie in quiet expectancy. It's a rare day when the Big Men must wait their turn of fate.

"Ya bastards need a straw man we can both trust, who can exchange me gold for US currency. This is MY deal. My straw man will get small, regular deliveries of gold coin, which he launders through your bank for cash. He banks the money in anonymous accounts of my choosing and lends it to you. You make payments to the account. The straw man will be the only link between me and you. You get the almighty cash flow you need to survive this depression, and then you leave me the 'ell alone. An' there's one other thing. From this point on, you'll be givin' the co-op members the same packing shed pricin' you give them big farms. That's the deal. Take it or leave it. You can have your man bring me your answer tomorrow."

Feeling the power of having them in his grasp, he reached into their private space on the table. "An' I'll be takin' that bottle of rum with me."

Driftwood turned to the door blocked by the Hun and said to him, "Step aside, you sorry sack o' shit." His twinkling blue and brown eyes bid the Big Men, adieu.

CHAPTER XIV
Buried Deep, Forgotten Long

"Rufus, I got somethin' I need to tell you. A while back, I was pickin' oysters in a creek bottom back of my place, when I found three wood and iron chests full of gold coins, pirate gold from a long time ago."

"Pirate. How you know dat?"

"Cause I talked to em a 'couple o nights ago, chewin' de root with Doctor Snake."

"Talk'um! But dey's graveyard dead, Missa Cory. How you gwine talk'um dead men?"

"Ghosts. They came right out of a green, smoky dream an' told me all about how they came by the gold, and how it got here, and what they want me to do with it."

"Say what? I en't want nothin' t' do wid no ghos'."

Driftwood pulled a handful of shiny gold coins from his pocket and spread them out on Rufus' kitchen table.

"Gawd 'amighty, Missa Cory. You's in big trouble if'n de Sheriff an 'e friends fine out 'bout dat gold."

"That's what the trial was all about. They tried to beat it out o' me, and when I wouldna' give it up, they set that mock trial to force me to buy me way out of jail with the gold. Rufus, you've been a good friend to me all these years. I never told you about the gold 'cause I knew it would bring you trouble."

"What you gwine do now?"

"That's why I'm here. I need your 'elp with a plan I have to put the gold to some good and keep us out o' trouble. Rufus, I'm trustin' you with me life.

"Dem ghos' plan? What you needs me do, Missa Cory?"

"Rufus, I need you to be me banker, me Straw Man. I need you to take the gold to the big bank in town a little bit at the time. The banker there will set up a special account, using a name only you and I know. He won't ask no questions, 'cause he's in it with the Sheriff and all their friends. The banker will sell the gold to private coin collectors and gold dealers and put the cash in this account. Then they'll borrow money from the account to keep the bank open, and to keep all their business interests afloat. They all need this money to survive this depression. It'll kill 'em to do it, but they have to pay us back with interest. Rufus, can you do this for me?"

"Dat sound dan'rous. What to keep 'em fum killin' bof us fo de gold?"

"They don't know where it is. And I'm not gonna tell you either, so they can't mess with you. We got 'em by the balls, Rufus, and they know it. And they sure don't want nobody knowing where they get their money, 'specially the Big Law."

"I's in wid you, Missa Cory."

"An' Rufus, you know that new house you been want'in to build for Jezebel? We gonna make the Sheriff and his friends pay for it."

"Missa Cory, payback for all dem hard times sho is fine. I ain't gots to talk'um no ghos' is I?"

Back in town the Big Men took their medicine when Driftwood broke down the details of the deal. They winced at the idea of being talked down to by an island bum, but they knew it was the best deal they were going to get. Driftwood knew even a bad dog won't bite the hand that feeds him.

The plan worked out remarkably well for the next several years. Rufus made the bank run once a month. The banker laundered the gold discreetly through private collectors and foreign exchanges. The Big Mens' financial interests survived the Great Depression. All seemed well on the surface, but long-held resentments simmered.

Far away in Washington DC, a file was started at the Office of the Treasury, a file to trace unusually large amounts of relic gold coin being sold out of a small southern town at the end of nowhere.

Across the Atlantic Ocean in Dublin, Ireland, an anonymous cable and bank draft opened a new account at The Bank of England. The cable read: "The House of Commons is to manage this account for the building of a memorial to the 34th Tyneside Irish Brigade, commemorating all those lads lost in the Great War. Deposits monthly. Work in faith."

The letter was signed, "One o' your'n".

CHAPTER XV
The Storm

Hurricanes were a fact of life along the South Carolina coast. With historic regularity, they well up in the eastern Atlantic Ocean and follow ocean currents across the equatorial Atlantic to make landfall on the east coast of the Americas, shaping times, places, and people.

The Great Storm of 1893 was particularly destructive to the Lowcountry. The storm made landfall at Savannah, Georgia on a seasonal high tide. The counter clockwise rotation of one hundred and thirty mile per hour winds pushed a twenty-foot wall of seawater surging over the Sea Islands. Thousands of people on remote islands drowned. The water was two stories high in downtown Beaufort, South Carolina.

A late summer day in 1940 began with an increased sea breeze blowing from the south. The sea oats atop the dunes on Harbor Island bowed in unison in the strengthening gale. It continued throughout the day and into the night, bringing a different taste to the air, sweet and heavy. The unsettled cows huddled together in a group in the densest thicket they could find, shoulder to shoulder, heads outward, eyes wide white with fear, searching for the oncoming evil they could not see. The horses whinnied and darted back and forth about their enclosures, trying to outrun their onrushing panic. A driving rain began lashing the islands in heavy squall bands. Palmetto trees knelt before the will of their master. The receding tide did not go low, and the waters soon began to rise. An old woman living next to Rufus Fripp remarked, "Da debil' in my bon's say a bad stom' a comin."

The beast had drawn its first breath from the sweaty, pained, and tortured West coast of Africa. Hungrily, it moved out over the Atlantic Ocean, feeding off the warm ocean currents, drawing increasing strength with a low and wistful moan. It spiraled its way west across the Azores sucking the life out of Haiti and Cuba, and everything in its path before turning north, along the East coast of North America. Like feral lightning seeking hard ground, it bobbed and weaved along the coast, hunting its prey.

Everyone on the islands began covering their doors and windows against the onslaught. Radio weather reports relied mostly upon information from ships at sea, but few homes had radios or telephones, so there was no way to know what was coming. There were no storm shelters, so some families huddled in churches. The shrimp boat captains all ran their boats far up into tight sheltered creeks they called 'hurricane holes' because the twisted, tree lined banks offered a small shield from the direct impact of storm winds.

The waters continued to rise as The Beast came closer. Hurricane tidewater swept over the Harbor Island causeway in pounding cataracts, washing away huge chunks of asphalt roadbed, severing it from the larger islands. The shrimp docks and heading sheds were waist deep in water, many with missing roofs.

The Beast had found its mark and Driftwood and Masie were stranded. Driftwood knew they were in trouble when the waters began coming under the door of their shack, and the winds had not eased. The worst was still to come, as the calm eye of the storm had not yet passed.

Pounding bands of wind and rain became a steady roar, louder with each life-threatening wave. Her eyes were wide with terror; Masie's screams were snatched from her throat before reaching Driftwood. The roofing tin whipped and rattled as if demon possessed, when, with a final death blow, the house gave in to a greater power, and its roof ripped away into the darkness.

The storm fast upon them, Driftwood grabbed a flashlight and coil of rope. They had to find higher ground further into the island. When he opened the front door, it was instantly snatched off its hinges and was gone. He tied the rope around their waists and stepped out into the torrent of waist deep water, fighting their way across the submerged highway and into the woods, bending headlong into the wind to keep from being blown off their feet and swept away. The bouncing flashlight beam was lost in the maelstrom of flying debris, tree limbs, and slashing rain.

The dense palmetto thickets of the inner island offered some relief from the winds. Driftwood and Masie found a large Live Oak tree and huddled on its lee side. Here, at least, they could hear each other talk. Masie prayed and Driftwood cursed. No manmade power could fight this enemy. The steady torrents and rising waters meant they could no longer stay on the ground. The mighty oak tree offered a saddle between outstretching limbs about eight feet off the ground. Driftwood cradled Masie's feet in his cupped hands and lifted her up to the crotch in the tree, scrambling up behind her.

The storm wound a bit tighter, it's full strength was nigh. Pine trees fell like pick-up-sticks, tree tops snapped off mid-height. Then he heard it. Like rolling thunder it came, the storm surge was upon them, hunting, hungry. In desperation, Driftwood tied them both to an oak limb and braced for impact. It hit them like a shell burst in "no mans' land", pinning them to the tree with a force strong enough to tear away their clothes and pound the breath from their lungs. A loud cracking noise came from the oak, and suddenly they were tumbling in the flotsam-filled backwash maw of the monster. Rolling with the maelstrom, Driftwood and Masie clutched each other while struggling to get their heads above the water for a life-saving breath of air. Their desperate eyes locked together in a knowing last embrace, they were slammed against a submerged tree and torn apart.

When Driftwood came up for air, he was alone, bleeding, unable to see for the rain stinging his face. "Masie, MASIEEEE!!!". There was only the wind roaring in response.

The eye of the storm passed over the island with an eerie calm; blue skies, no rain or wind, the Beast well fed. Only the high water of the storm surge remained, ready to drain to the sea the detritus of its feeding. Driftwood fearfully stumbled through the tattered woods hollering for Masie. When the backside of the storm crossed the island, it was only a slightly weaker mate to the initial blow. Flood waters subsided leaving the carnage behind. The Harbor Island road and surrounding dunes were littered with busted pine trees, uprooted palmettos, and a forty-foot sailboat lodged ten feet off the ground in some cedar trees.

Across the islands, other homes were heavily damaged, or no longer there. Rufus lost a horse and two cows. There were two other lives lost to the flood waters.

Alone, out on his Horseshoe Point, a heart-broken Driftwood Cory cried out his pain into the night. His Masie was gone. He was all alone again in the world, save for the company of his demons.

CHAPTER XVI
Yellow Glows its Siren Song

Driftwood was never the same after losing Masie to the storm of 1940. His hair a little grayer, the stooped shoulders of resignation a little more pronounced. Life was slowly wearing him down. Defiant and indefatigable in his youth, the new reality was more about hanging on than moving forward.

He did rebuild the shack. If there was a silver lining in the aftermath of the storm, it was that the beaches were littered with debris from tourists' beach homes. Replacement doors, windows, and lumber were his for the taking. He even managed to find a small gas-powered generator in one destroyed building. Electric power, if he wanted it, was an upgrade from the kerosene lamps and wood stove from before. But the rebuilt home was lonely and cold without his Masie.

137

The causeway to the mainland was rebuilt with two lanes. In 1941 the State of South Carolina bought Hunting Island from a group of sportsmen who owned it as a retreat for hunting deer, duck, and wild boar. A new bridge was built connecting Hunting Island to Harbor Island, and the former hunting retreat later became a State park.

World War II came and went. By 1946 the increased access to the islands became both a blessing and a curse. Driftwood's monthly stipend for access across Horseshoe Point to the State's lighthouse barge was cut off with the new road offering easier, faster service. On the other hand, motor access to Hunting Island's beaches brought legions of beachgoers and the surfing crowd.

Increased tourist traffic was an up-tick for Driftwood's minimalist lifestyle. More tourists bought more driftwood carvings and horseshoe crab masks. The new breed of risk-taking surfers found a kindred soul in Driftwood. Mostly teenagers, they thumbed rides to the beach with older friends who had driving licenses. They weren't old enough to drink beer or liquor, but a little subtle back door trading worked out well for all concerned. The surfers stopped at Driftwood's shack on their way to the beach, "for a wee taste" of island moonshine. In return, they brought Driftwood interesting finds washed up on the beach from all over the world. Hand-made Portuguese fish net floats always sold well, as did unusual sea shells, sharks teeth, nature's own carving of unique driftwood pieces, and even the occasional sea turtle shell. Driftwood also offered a few basic beach-going essentials, like suntan lotion, cold soft drinks, and boiled peanuts.

The Big Men opened a modern seafood restaurant and bar on Harbor Island, directly across the highway from Driftwood's place. It was called the Johnson Creek Tavern (or "JCT"). On a wall just inside the front door of

JCT's hung an aerial photo of the island and nearby marshes. A 1954 tax map photo showed the roof of Driftwood's shack. It also showed Driftwood's treasure spot, way out back from Horseshoe Point. For all their lust and greed for Driftwood's gold, and the years of resentful frustration at their inability to learn where he hid it, a treasure map to all their dreams hung inside their very own front door.

Driftwood's business was good enough to satisfy his minimal material needs. He became an island icon. A white-haired gnome, sitting out front of his shack beneath a palmetto tree beside the road, spending a typical day carving on something to sell, nodding and waving to tourists passing by. Parents with their children stopped by for a candy tart and to hear him tell tall tales in his Irish brogue.

"Aye, lad, what's that I see in yer ear?" With a deft snap of his wrist and roll of those two toned sparkling eyes, Driftwood pulled a shiny gold coin from the child's ear.

"This ere's me lucky piece. I'll trade ya for a coin of the realm," he said, pocketing the shiny bauble in return for a case quarter. "Have yer Pop pick you out a sweet."

All the while, as many things on the islands were changing, some deeper, darker things stayed the same. Once each month Driftwood used the cover of darkness to leave Horseshoe Point in his bateau, returning an hour later and ten pounds heavier than when he left. Once each month a more prosperous Rufus Fripp stopped by in his big black Cadillac on his straw run to the bank in town. Ten pounds of Spanish gold coin was worth a hundred times the market value of gold, now at forty-five dollars per ounce. That was big money when an average working man's salary was six hundred dollars per year. The Big Men financed their greed. Anonymous bank drafts continued to cross the Atlantic. Driftwood's private war with reality went on unabated. The ageless Dr. Snake, some said nearly a hundred years old, went quietly about his business of shaping, shifting, and manipulating the middle gray social buffer between Gullah culture and The Man.

Post-war growth and development in Beaufort County between the 1950's and 1960's was explosive. The Big Men had big plans. Plans for future highway projects seemed to find their way to cigar smoked back rooms and morning breakfast meetings before being made public. Quiet real estate transactions magically locked in huge profits. A small hardware store in town secured the seemingly impossible contract to provide all the miles of water piping and pump stations, bringing drinking water to town from the Savannah River, thirty miles away. An absentee owner of Harbor Island managed to outmaneuver the EPA in getting permits to illegally dredge marshlands, creating a hundred new, deep water lots.

In 1961 a private developer came to town with the idea of developing Fripp Island, the next uninhabited barrier island south of Hunting Island, and namesake of colonial planter and former pirate, Captain John Fripp. Never mind there was no road through Hunting Island to get there, or even a bridge to cross Fripp Inlet. He was visionary in his passionate pleas to the Big Men who owned the island.

On the way back from one of his daydreaming trips to the south end of Hunting Island, the developer stopped at Driftwood's shack for a cold RC Cola. He took a break in the shade of a Palmetto tree, casually noting the "little bit of everything" hanging around. Driftwood sat silently under the porch cover, bare foot in khaki shorts and a sun-faded tie-died T- shirt. Patching a shrimp net, missing nothing, his gnarled and practiced fingers deftly wove intricate knots while eyeing the newcomer.

With a ringing spit of tobacco chaw into the bucket at his feet, Driftwood opined, "Been seein' you runnin' back and forth up this road all week long. What's your game, laddy buck?"

"Well, old timer—"

"Name's Driftwood," he interrupted with a sweep of his hand.

"Well, Driftwood, I got me a big idea about Fripp Island. Been watching it from the end of Hunting Island, thinking about making it a special place to live, with a golf course, beach houses, cook-outs on the beach, and beautiful sunsets. I need a ride to the island. You got a boat?"

"Sixteen-footer, tied out back to the point."

"What'd you take to row me to Fripp? I want to lay down some boot leather. Need to see what I can't see from the map of the place."

"Well, Sonny, that's a two-tide trip. How about twenty-five dollars and you throw in the 'what-fors.'"

"Done."

"'What-fors'?"

"That'd be a case of cold beer for ME, mate, and WHATEVER for you! Be here, at seven tomorrow morning, sharp."

"Okay, seven sharp. And Driftwood, the name's Jack, Jack Killian."

Daylight came on a light breeze from the southeast, pushing billowy clouds glowing pink in the rising sun. The tide had just started to flood when

Driftwood and the developer left the dock at Horseshoe Point. A motor boat would have been faster, but the developer wanted to experience the trip the old way. After all, it was old time plantation charm that he was planning to sell to "come h'yer" Yankees wanting a place in the sun.

Driftwood pulled hard on the weathered, hand-carved oak oars, creaking in their leather-bound locks. The light skiff fairly flitted across the waves. Made of quarter-inch marine plywood on a driftwood frame, the bateau was lighter than its cargo. During the three-hour row up Johnson Creek to Harbor River and out the mouth of Story River, they passed a 'gator slide coming off the back of Hunting Island, a couple of curious deer on the woods edge, and hundreds of water birds leaving island roosts for salt water feeding grounds. A nervous osprey screamed its resentment at the passing bateau from its overhead nest atop a lone pine tree.

A pod of dolphins nosed alongside the skiff, close enough to touch. Driftwood calling them by name caused a start from the developer.

"Jock, Joe, you're a long way from Horseshoe Point this mornin'."

"You got names for those dolphins?"

"Aye, friends of mine. Always try to save 'em somethin' from me nets. They make fine company and always got a smile upon their faces. Better'n most people I know."

At the mouth of Story River, Driftwood pulled into a small marsh hammock and beached the skiff.

"We'll tie off here 'till the tide turns. Then we can ride 'er out to the sound and the North end of yer' island. Find yerself a spot in the shade, an' pass me one of them cold beers, will ya, mate?"

Not much was said between the two. The developer was lost in his daydreams about Fripp Island. Driftwood nodded off, his head on a palmetto log and beer froth in his beard, asleep in minutes. He tied his tide clock to his right big toe; the tide clock being a piece of string tied at the other end to the boat. When the tide began to ebb, it would pull his toe and wake him for the last leg of the trip.

After an hour nap, the pair shoved off into the outgoing tide. They made Fripp beach in an hour. The developer took off down the beach with his maps and a compass. Driftwood hung a small tarp over a driftwood tripod for sun shelter and layered a dozen green palmetto fronds for a bed.

Six hours later, the developer returned, excited over his discoveries.

Driftwood was passed out from twelve beers.

The developer cast his dreams to the wind and the senseless Driftwood.

"Wide beaches, high, broad dune fields, and a thousand acres of high land. Even a sweet water pond. Turtle crawls on the beach, and deer tracks everywhere. Paradise. Got to do something about those damn wild hogs, though. I can just see some old blue haired Yankee woman screaming down the beach ahead of a pack of pigs, just when I'm trying to sell her husband some real estate."

It would be dark soon. Driftwood awoke, started a fire and cut a long slender branch, which he sharpened on one end.

"What's that for, Driftwood?" asked the developer.

"Dinner," he replied, ambling off into the sunset.

Odd little man, mused the developer as he pulled out a can of Spam and a waxed paper stick of Saltine Crackers for his dinner.

An hour later Driftwood came lolling back to the fire with a pocket full of sea turtle eggs, some fresh clams, and eight large blue crabs, "finned" and looped onto his stick. He had used the slender stick to probe several turtle nests until he found one the 'coons hadn't raided. He only took six of the hundred eggs in the nest. Need, not greed. The crabs he speared in swirl holes around tree stumps. He would see the florescent eye stalks of the crabs peeking above the sand they buried themselves in. A sharp jab, one inch behind the eyes, speared them mid body. Then he took an opposite third leg on each side and crossed the crab's body, wedging the pointy end into the joint of the opposing big claw. Ditto the other side. The crab was stuck cross armed, and ready to slide onto the carrying pole.

Driftwood buried the turtle eggs in the hot sand of the fire pit to poach, while raking out a bed of coals to steam his crabs and clams. No pot, no problem. They would steam in their own shells. Knock back a couple of cold beers and it was "Good night, Irene".

The developers' Spam and crackers seemed a little lacking in comparison.

Sunrise brought a reverse of the previous day's trip. The developer left Driftwood's shack with a head full of dreams, and a new respect for the old saying about judging a book by its cover. The developer never realized he'd eaten Spam and crackers with his future banker, driving past Driftwoods humble shack every trip into town.

Conventional capital sources for a bold idea of developing a wild barrier island like Fripp were nonexistent in the 1960's. The negotiated price for Fripp Island with the Big Men who owned it was $500,000. The bridge would cost another $300,000, according to an estimate from the South Carolina Department of Transportation (DOT). Then there was the cost of infrastructure, men, and equipment.

"This is financial folly, a pipe dream," said local townsfolk. A pipe dream with a big payday, if it could be pulled off. There was money to be made on real estate speculation, and income from the construction company, the insurance business, and the banking businesses the Big Men controlled. Off the books, the deal was struck with handshakes and a round of drinks, while the black Cadillac kept making the monthly trips to town.

Rufus Fripp was a frugal man of few vices. Being a deacon of the First African Baptist Church, he was a filter for avaricious temptations. There was, though, one innocent pleasure he indulged in. Rufus loved his Cadillac, always clean and freshly polished. It had one subtle improvement not visible from the outside.

Rufus had a nephew who worked as a diesel mechanic, maintaining the big engines of shrimp trawlers. He also worked on cars as a sideline. Rufus had him replace the caddy's original engine with Cadillac's new 390 cubic inch monster engine. It was bored, stroked, and fed through two big bore Holley four-barrel carburetors. His big black caddy could fly.

The wealth and prosperity of Beaufort County began to attract regional interests in the early 1960's. The Big Bank flourished. Share prices soared and fortunes made. The engine of all this prosperity remained deeply hidden in a separate vault below the chairman's office. Newcomers were good for business in general, but outsiders brought new ideas and ways of doing business, not always in tune with the interests of the Big Men. Too much scrutiny had a way of curbing their appetites. They couldn't continue to play so fast and loose with the rules. Such was the offer, by a large regional banking chain, to buy up the shares of the Big Bank in a merger. Stock prices would triple. Millions of dollars of new wealth would fill the Big Men's coffers. They would have to find new ways of doing business and cut loose some old ties.

A bank merger also meant detailed audits, which could threaten everything the Big Men had built over the last twenty years. No one could ever know their empire was built on the back of a river bum and his illicit gold. Long held, seething resentments would come out. No one could ever be allowed to know their secrets.

Driftwood Cory had to disappear.

On a blustery Sunday morning in March of 1963, a gray sedan made a slow pass in front of Driftwood Driftwood's shack. A Molotov cocktail concoction of kerosene and gasoline burst against the front wall, and the car raced away. Sun dried beach timbers caught fire quickly, to crackle and snap in the quickly growing flames. Inside the shack, the habitually hung-over Driftwood slept on in demon slumber.

Towering columns of thick, black smoke from burning asphalt roof shingles could be seen two miles away on Hunting Island beach, where a couple of teenage surfers were waking from an overnight beach party.

"Man, we got to haul ass. Our folks are gonna be pissed. We were supposed to be home last night."

"You better start thinking about how we're gonna talk ourselves out of this one. It was your idea man, and we didn't even get laid."

"What say you and me stop by ole Driftwood's place for a quick shot of that stump poison he makes? Hell, we can't get in any more trouble than we're already in."

Rounding the Johnson Creek Bridge the two young surfers could see the fire consuming Driftwood's shack. There were no fire trucks, no police, nothing. Johnson Creek Tavern was closed, no one in the parking lot on a Sunday morning.

"Damn it, kick in the door."

"Driftwood, hey, Driftwood, you in here?"

The thick, choking smoke engulfed them. When they got to the back room, Driftwood, also overcome by smoke, was on the floor. The boys threw a chair through the back window, followed by a limp Driftwood Cory. Once out into clean air, they collapsed, heaving for air. Then the roof caved in and the whole structure fell in on itself. Within an hour, there was nothing left of the shack but a pile of cinders and a horseshoe crab mask nailed to a nearby pine tree.

The boys dropped Driftwood off at the hospital in town before calling their parents. All three suffered from smoke inhalation. After a brief examination the doctor declared, "Driftwood's gonna make it. He's a little singed around the edges, but not enough to cook the ole geezer. Good thing his liquor breath didn't catch fire! Lucky you boys got there when you did."

The weight of the moment got the boys off the hook with their parents.

Arson was suspected, but not seriously looked into by the Sheriff's department. "That old fool burnt his own shack down," was the gist of the brief incident report.

The boys visited Driftwood in the hospital the next day, snuck him a half-pint from the stash he kept hidden behind his shack.

"We saw the Sheriff's deputy parked under the Johnson Creek Bridge when your place burned. He had to see what was happening, but he never moved. When we got you out of the house the car was gone."

The good news of Driftwood's surviving the fire met a different reception in town.

CHAPTER XVII
The Reckoning

It had been said that the most powerful human emotion is neither love, nor fear, nor hope. It is hate; cold, hard hate. Hatred of enemies, hatred of one's self, or hatred of unbridled power can push a wounded man to new strength; it can embolden him to charge the guns of war. A fighter known to rise up for one more round, Ian Hugh "Driftwood" Cory had seen and experienced both, and more, in his lifetime. Three days out of the hospital following his attempted murder, Driftwood was bent on demanding a reckoning from those who had tormented and harassed him for so many years.

New found strength moved him to action.

Rufus Fripp brought Driftwood back from the hospital to stay with him while he recovered from the fire that almost took his life.

"There'll be time enough to rebuild me house. The shit's about to hit the fan, mate. That sheriff has buggered me for the last time"

"What you 'bout t' do, Missa Cory?"

"I drafted this letter for you to hold, should something happen to me. It explains the last forty years, how I found the gold, our straw man plans to get some good from it without unleashing all the pain that much treasure can cause. It tells about how the Big Men financed their lies, and it says what I want done with the money I've been sending back to Ireland all these years. You keep this letter safe, Rufus. If they know the truth is outside their reach, they won't come after you the way they did me. It's already addressed, all you got to do is mail it. Rufus, you got enough money saved up to take care of your family?"

"An' den sum."

"Good. We're goin' t' town tomorrow to set things right."

The next morning the big black Cadillac that had made so many gold runs over the last twenty years made one last ride to the Big Bank, arriving just as the front doors were unlocked.

"Rufus, I need you to park directly in front of the bank and wait for me to come out. Keep your eye out for the Sheriff or the Hun. If I make it out of the bank in one piece, they'll be none too happy about it. They won't try nothin' in the bank, and with you right here on the open street with folks all around, they won't have no chance out here either."

"I bees ri' che wid de motor runnin'."

"Make sure you feed the meter. Don't give 'em no cause to mess with you."

Driftwood stepped out of the caddy and over to the public phone booth outside the Big Bank. He made a long-distance call, collect.

"Hello?"

"Yes, this is the Department of the Treasury. May I help you?"

"I've a story to tell ye about money laundering and stolen gold."

Driftwood's call was readily accepted, no charge. The Treasury Department had been quietly stalking the source of large, regular amounts of unregistered gold entering dealer markets over the years. There were rules and regulations; proper disclosures for dealing in gold. Antiquities and archaeological finds could belong to the State. Yes, they certainly were interested.

Like gardeners searching for the nest hole of yellow jackets, the agents watched from a distance, noting a single wasp here, two crossing the same flight path there, then three, five, and ten. Tightening the search circle would eventually lead them to the entrance hole, cleverly hidden under a rock or lawn fixture. Driftwood's tip was the call that finally closed the net.

Ten minutes later Driftwood walked into the Big Bank, past the tellers, to the doubled doored Chairman's office.

The head teller challenged him. "You there! Who are you, and what's your business here?"

"Tell the boss man Driftwood is here to see him."

The head teller knocked on the office door and entered.

"Sir, there's a crotchety old bum out here demanding to see you. He says he has business with you. He calls himself Driftwood. What do you want me to do?"

"Give me two minutes, then show him in."

The banker picked up his phone, made a hurried call. When finished, he pressed the button on his door buzzer and allowed Driftwood to enter.

Without any small talk, Driftwood took command of the meeting from the flustered banker.

"I'm here for me money, to close me accounts. I want it all, and right now."

"What are you talking about, sir?"

"Me money. The money you and your friends have suckled on for the last twenty years. You'll get it now or I'll call the Big Law down on you. You'll all burn. Money laundering, extortion, and attempted murder is illegal, don't ya know."

"Mr. Driftwood, I can't possibly do that in a single transaction. That's six million dollars! That's more money than all the recorded deposits of the bank! I can't possibly reconcile a withdrawal of that size."

"Not me problem. I want it in a cashier's check made out to The Bank of England. I've drafted a letter detailin' all our dealin's these last many years and left it in good hands. It'll be mailed today if'n I don't leave with me money. You and your associates can cover the check or go to jail. If'n it was me, I know which I'd be choosin'."

"Okay, okay! Allow me a few minutes to get the paperwork."

The Big Banker called in his son, the Vice President of the bank. "Will, I need you to prepare a certified check according to these instructions. Just do it. I'll explain everything later."

Meanwhile, the High Sheriff groused over the banker's call of a few moments earlier. Speaking to no one in particular, he fumed, "Goddamn it! That sorry, weak-kneed, bastard, sumbitch. If he cashes out that account, we all burn."

The Sheriff called the city attorney. "We got an emergency. Driftwood is down at the bank demanding his money, the money we don't have! He's threatening to turn us in to the Feds if he doesn't get it. I can keep the lid on things here in my county, but I got no pull with the Feds. They'd love to see me go down. And you'd fall, too, along with all the others. If he cashes that check, we'll have to liquidate everything we own to cover it. And if we don't, the IRS will chew us new assholes. Who knows what the FBI would have to say about it. The upcoming bank merger will go sour, too. That's another couple million up in smoke."

"Driftwood's not as easy as we played him for. I guess he's pissed about your man burning his shack down around him."

"No shit. I should have made sure of it myself; toasted the little bastard. Then we wouldn't have this problem."

"What's your plan, Sheriff?"

"My plan? We're all in this together. We can't let him cash that check! That's the plan."

The bank was hushed by the sight of the Big Banker's flushed face and sweaty palms. Bank patrons turned to one another in awkward whispers. The head teller scurried about and returned with the certified check

153

for six million dollars. The banker's son had a stunned look on his face.

"Sir? Dad!"

"Not now, son, not now".

Five minutes later Driftwood left the banker's office. With the sweet taste of vengeance served up cold, he taunted, "It's been a pleasure doin' business with you, sir."

Driftwood quickly exited the bank, canvassing the street for the trouble he knew was surely coming, before hopping into the purring caddy.

"Got it. Quick, to the Post Office."

The Big Banker's desperate face pressed against the bank's front widow to watch the black caddy drive away with their money, and the evidence that could put them in prison for a long time.

Driftwood pulled two envelopes from his breast pocket, both addressed to The Bank of England, Dublin, Ireland. One contained instructions and the certified check for six million dollars; the other, another message.

"Here's the plan, Rufus. I'm goin' to mail this one from here in town. You circle the block several times to make sure you ain't bein' followed. Then drive this other envelope to Savannah and mail it from the big Post Office on Broad Street. Make sure nobody follows you. The High Sheriff might be able to intercept mail here in town, but not across the state line in a big town like Savannah. He ain't got no mojo in Georgia. Then you get back home like nothin' happened. I'll hitch a ride back to your house."

"Missa Cory, watch out fo' yosef. You 'member what I say 'bout messin' wit de High Sheriff."

Rufus pulled away from the Post Office, his eyes on the rear-view mirrors. Driftwood mailed the first envelope and, leaving by the side door of the Post Office, quickly worked his way through side alleys to the other side of town, out of sight of everyone but stray cats. While he was sitting at the bridge foot with his thumb out for a hitch, the Sheriff's patrol car pulled up to the Post Office.

The High Sheriff carried a warrant, signed by the Judge for the City Attorney, to intercept mail he said was evidence of a crime. In violation of Federal law, the Post Master quickly handed it over. Rules are rules, but he knew who ran this town. The never-publicly-flustered High Sheriff pocketed the letter and hastened to a meeting of the Big Men in the Attorney's office.

"Did you get it?" asked one of them.

"Well, man, open it. What's it say?"

The High Sheriff carefully tore the end seam of the envelope and pulled out a letter. His face went red with anger. "God, dddamnit!!" he stuttered, and threw it onto the table.

The City Attorney picked up the letter, and smiling at the irony of the situation, he read aloud,

> *"Old Driftwood knows,*
> *Of Big Mens' woes,*
> *Money found, heaven sent,*
> *Fevered greed, and fevered spent.*
> *All a bouncing to Hell's gate go."*

The sheriff's temper exploded. "That limey bastard screwed us. He faked us out chasing this letter. The real letter with the check must still be with Rufus. If he can't mail it here, he's got to go out of town."

"Sheriff, you stop that man any way you can," admonished a cool, confident Big John, unaccustomed to loss of control in any situation.

"There's only one road in and out of town. I'll radio ahead to one of my deputies to block the road at Gardens Corner, looking for a nigger in a big, black Cadillac."

CHAPTER XVIII
Rufus

By the time the Sheriff left his meeting with the Big Men, Rufus had made it out of the city limits and half way to Gardens Corner on the coastal highway to Savannah. He was staying just under the 60-mph speed limit, careful not to attract attention, when he saw a fast approaching car sporting a domed roof light in his rear-view mirror. The sheriff's deputy was coming on hard as both cars reached the Gardens Corner turn. Tight on Rufus' bumper, the deputy flipped on the blue light and flashed his headlights, signaling Rufus to pull over. Rufus, a big grin on his face, took a firm grip on the steering wheel as he fish tailed the big caddy through the turn and stomped down on the accelerator of the big 390. "Les jes'see how big yours' be, missa sheriff de-pu-te.'"

The deputy's Dodge Police Interceptor was hot on his ass. Nose to tail, they careened down the two-lane road faster and faster; seventy miles per hour, eighty, ninety. The deputy pulled alongside the caddy, trying to bump him off the road. For nearly five miles they bumped and banged, each trying to unseat the other.

"I got you now you, boy." The road opened up on the ten-mile straight toward the Georgia line. Rufus leaned hard on the big caddy. When the second four-barrel carburetor on the big 390 opened up with an air gulping roar, the caddy lunged forward, unleashing a full five hundred horsepower. One hundred miles per hour, one-fifteen, one-twenty, one-forty! And gone! Nothing but blue smoke and fast disappearing taillights.

The deputy pounded his fists on the dash and grabbed the radio mic. "Damn! Sheriff, I lost him. I don't know what that caddies got under the hood, but he can flat, fucking fly. I was pedaling as fast as I could and he just walked away from me. He must've been doing a hundred and fifty. What 'chu want me to do now, Sheriff?"

"Damnit! Stake out Garden's Corner. He's got to come home sometime. Maybe I should send yo' mamma out there to get him."

Rufus' escape was not welcome news to the Big Men. They were up against it now. There was nothing to do but mortgage all they owned to cover the check. Otherwise the bank would fold, and their secret would get out.

When word got back to the Big Banker, he dropped the phone, face pale with beaded sweat and grabbed his left arm. A deep piercing pain shot through his chest. He was ruined, his family reputation in tatters. His family bank would fail. All would be lost. He staggered out of his office into the teller area and stumbled to the floor, dead, felled by a massive heart attack.

Back in Savannah, having safely mailed his package, Rufus whittled the day away, waiting for nightfall. He knew the coastal road would be watched. What the Sheriff's deputies didn't think about was the labyrinth of dirt farm roads paralleling the main highway. Rufus knew these roads well, having routinely trucked out small farmers' crops to market for the co-op. By five a.m. a sleepy patrol officer called in from his stakeout.

"Sheriff, ain't nobody come down this road in a black Cadillac or anything else since 11 o'clock last night."

Like Brer Rabbit in the briar patch, Rufus slipped past the blockade, and with lights out, crossed the bridge back onto his island. He was home in time to catch breakfast with Driftwood.

CHAPTER XIX
Revenge

Nine o'clock the next morning the High Sheriff and City Attorney arrived at the Big Bank to investigate the Banker's death. Routine enough, under normal circumstances, this time they had another agenda. "Our asses are in the hot seat. If Driftwood's check to The Bank of England gets cashed, all hell is going to break loose. We gotta move fast."

The Sheriff sealed the Banker's office, demanding the Banker's son, the Vice President, provide the combination to the private vault. The Sheriff and City Attorney rifled through the vault, purging it of any documents tying them to the gold laundering scheme that had made them rich men those last twenty years. They left a paper trail pointing to the Banker and his son.

The same day the Big Men took out a large loan from a bank in Charleston in the exact amount of Driftwood's withdrawal. After a little shady paperwork their secret was safe. The fix was in.

Two days later, three suits, showing badges from Atlanta, showed up at the Sheriff's office.

"We're from the United States Treasury Office, here to investigate reports of illegal money laundering. We have Federal search warrants for this list of people we need to talk to, including you, Sheriff. Don't leave town."

The Feds spent the entire week on a full audit of the bank's records and business dealings. While normally satisfied to expose typical small-town cronyism and collect a few fines, they were, this time hunting for scalps. Illegal gold, and lots of it, had been trafficking out of this bank for years. They were interviewed by the local newspaper editor trying to string a story together from all the frantic speculation flying about town. Locals began to close their accounts, adding to the bank's cash flow problems.

The Feds put their cards on the table. The front page of *The Beaufort Gazette* began with; "Somebody is going to Federal Prison!"

The Big Men met to make sure they told the same story. No one knew anything about any gold. They just assumed the Big Banker had legitimate access to the capital he lent them for their various business ventures.

Each of the Big Men was separately interviewed by the Feds. Their story held up to scrutiny. At the end of the investigation, all available evidence pointed solely to the Big Banker, and by association, his son, as the guilty parties.

After a quick ride out to the Island to interview a rummy island bum, no one believed the allegation that Driftwood could pull off a scheme as elaborate as what they were told.

"All I know is the rumor on the street. I don't know where they got the gold. Ask the Banker."

Rufus was quietly left outside the investigation. The Big Men definitely did not want the Feds talking to their bag man.

Since they couldn't jail a dead man, they sent the Bankers son to Federal prison for five years, mostly because his signature was on many of the bank ledgers, "Doing Time for Daddy's Crime". The bank was fined for illegal accounting activity and put into the supervisory charge of outside regulators.

When the dust-up over the Federal Investigation settled, the Big Men found themselves desperate for cash. They had to mortgage all their holdings to indemnify the bank's bottom line and get the Feds off their backs. They also needed to find the rest of the gold. By their estimation, there should have been at least another five hundred pounds of gold in Driftwood's stash, if they could believe his claim of three thousand pounds twenty years earlier. At the exchange rate of the Banker's last transaction, that was almost two and a half million dollars. They could find another market for the gold if they could only get their hands on it.

In a smoky meeting of the Big Men, they weighed their options.

"Sheriff, beating the gold out of Driftwood didn't work the first time. With his home and woman gone, he's nothing left to lose. We got no leverage there."

"Maybe so, but Rufus Fripp is another story. Rufus drove the gold into town every month. He gave Driftwood food and shelter. He built a nice new house, squeezing our asses in this deal. And, deputy, he whipped your butt in that souped-up Cadillac of his. I'll bet my badge Rufus knows where Driftwood has the gold hid."

The Sheriff's lapdog deputy stood up from his seat in the corner.

"Sheriff, I've been doing your dirty work all these years, for nothing but deputy pay. I never asked for much. Now, I know what you know. I'll get that gold for you, but I want a piece of the action this time. The Feds are watching all of you. They don't give a shit about me. I'm invisible."

All heads nodded in agreement around the room.

"Alright, Joe. Do what you have to. We win, you win. You get caught, you're on your own. Deal?"

The Hun agreed with a greasy, toothy grin, and slid from the room.

When he was gone, the City Attorney asked, "You think he can do it?"

"Either way this works out," said the Sheriff, exhaling a blue cigar smoke ring, "Joe's got to go. He's the only loose end we haven't tidied up."

The City Attorney shook his head and mused, "No wonder them nigahs call you the High Sheriff."

For the next few weeks Driftwood and Rufus laid low. They stayed out on the islands, working Rufus' fall crop of collard greens and turnips. They knew a storm was coming. "You don' go a pokin' yo' finger in de High Sheriff' eye and 'spect he to let it go," volunteered Rufus.

"Damn those Feds, Rufus. They were supposed to jail the whole cockeyed bunch of 'em. We served 'em up on a silver platter. How the hell did they get out of it?"

"Missa Cory, you ain't the fus'un t' try de High Sheriff. He gots lots o' enemies. He done got de debil on he side. Das what he gots. Folks in town say he done lay it off on de Banker, but he stiff daid. Folks don' call him de High Sheriff fo' nutin'."

"That leaves us back to where we started this whole mess, except now, they know who ratted them out. We got to keep a keen weather eye, Rufus. For sure as Saint Vidas' Curse, they'll be comin' for us."

CHAPTER XX
The Stand

The late 1960's were dangerous times in the South, particularly for the Gullah on the islands, who were the first to be freed from slavery by the public reading of the Emancipation Proclamation in Beaufort in 1863. White political power would never be the same. Resentments ran deep. The visit to Penn School by Dr. Martin Luther King in 1963 only served to re-open that old wound. Dr. King was at Penn School, the first school in the country for freed slaves, to re-energize his civil rights movement. It was there he wrote his famous speech, "I Have a Dream". His visit garnered national publicity, with news media covering the event from all over the country. The following Saturday was scheduled a public rally, speeches from prominent leaders in the movement, and a "walk for peace", led by Dr. King.

Rufus and Driftwood both attended the rally, both seeking redress of old hurts, but each marching under a different banner. Rufus marched for racial and political equality, for fairness in the workplace, and equal access to education. His people's grievances were well documented.

Driftwood's life was squeezed between two worlds, the one he left behind in the trenches of France, and the one he found at the end of a fated train ride to the Lowcountry Sea Islands. The freedom march was one way for Driftwood to stand up for the rights of his people, the downtrodden Irish, suffering under the thumb of indifferent British rule.

Many said the trouble with Ireland was that it had too many Irishmen. Since the days of the Norman Invasion, the Irish had stubbornly refused to be tamed by their British overlords. The British tried to tax them out. They tried to breed them out of existence with the overlords' "right of the first night" known as "jus primae noctis", whereby ruling nobleman took a new bride's virginity on her wedding night. "Mix the blood over time and we'll breed them out."

"We'll starve them out" became the cry. By the mid 1800's most Irish farmlands had been converted to raising beef for shipment to British markets. Plots leased to itinerant farmers by the landlord's middlemen kept getting squeezed smaller and smaller, until the only crop that could feed them was the potato. The potato became the dominant food staple for the country. Such sole reliance on a single food source was bound to cause problems. This came to pass on a massive scale between 1845 and 1854. Known as the Great Famine, the failure of the potato crop due to potato blight ravaged the land with disease, mass starvation, and emigration to other lands. Twenty-five percent of the population left Ireland for Europe and the New World. Indifference to this suffering by the British amounted to a policy of indirect genocide.

Rufus' and Driftwood's two worlds were so far apart, yet so familiar. Fate played no favorites.

There were few white faces in the crowd assembled for the freedom march, save for Driftwood and the sheriff's deputies ringing the crowd. There was energy in the air, a great anticipation of something great to come. Then, shouting over in the corner, a gunshot, and pandemonium. The sheriff's deputies tore into the crowd swinging their night sticks, kicking ass and not worrying with names. They singled Driftwood out for a beat down, kicking him on the ground as they thumped him with their sticks and leaded jacks. When Rufus came dragging a news cameraman with him, the deputies faded away. The swarming crowd moved past the beaten man on the ground, as does a stampeding herd of wildebeest leave a downed comrade to the lions on the Serengeti Plains of Africa.

The evening newscast reported the event as well managed by local law enforcement, with only a few scattered distractions. The marchers marched, Dr. King gave his speech, and went on to his death in Mississippi in 1968, felled by the assassin's bullet. The truth not only set Dr. King free; it made him a martyr to a worldwide generation seeking their "dreams".

CHAPTER XXI
Righteous

Fall's first cold snap signaled harvest time. Rufus and Driftwood joined the other local farmers in picking and boxing their produce for trucking to market.

"Missa Cory, you bes' be stayin' ritch'ere. No need fuh' you t' be showin' yo sef on de road. We gots plenty o' hands to off load at de railhead."

"An' you watch out, Rufus. Stay tight with the other trucks and don't you get off by yourself. You know the sheriff is gunnin' fer ye."

The co-op made its annual fall trip to market, a dozen trucks in all. It was an hour and a half drive, in the heavily laden convoy, from the islands to Yemassee, with Rufus, as head of the co-op, in the lead truck. Their mood was a happy one. Three months hard work was about to pay off. Life was a gamble for the small truck farmers. With every crop and every season, most of them put their entire net worth back into the ground as seed and fertilizer. Faith in the Lord, trust in each other, and hard work saw them through.

Thirty minutes outside of town, Rufus saw flashing headlights in the rear-view mirror. The trucks behind him were signaling something. Somebody break down? As Rufus eased into his brakes, a flash of blue and red of a Sheriff's car blasted past his truck. The cop car slowed down, pulled into traffic just ahead of Rufus, and turned his lights off. No siren; just a steady pacing of the caravan. The cruiser moved left and eased back alongside Rufus' truck, the Deputy on the passenger side nodding a dark, shaded stare. Then, just as suddenly, it turned left onto a side road and was gone. "Ain't no run'in wit de Man gwine come to no good," Rufus remarked. The nervous caravan drove on to the market.

The sale was good for the farmers. They all fetched top dollar for their crops, another crop in, another prayer answered. One of the men pulled a pint from under his seat and they passed it around the crowd gathered at the back of Rufus' truck. It wasn't the big Harvest Throw Down the plantation growers put on, but it was equally earned and equally satisfying to the Gullah farmers.

The ride home from market was normally uneventful. Turning a bend in the road, the caravan reached the earlier sheriff's cruiser stopped across the road ahead, lights flashing indicating a traffic stop. Hell, everybody knows farm trucks take a beating. Not one of them could pass a full safety inspection of every single taillight or blinker. But, like spitting on the sidewalk, no one paid much attention to harmless infractions, unless it involved an accident or something serious.

One by one, each truck was checked for registration, license, tags, and running lights. A young deputy passed out citations under the watchful eye of the Hun, leaning cross armed against the side of the patrol car. The sham inspection needed to appear routine, but the tediousness of it all chafed at the burning intensity in the Hun's dark shaded eyes, and a subtle nod toward Rufus' truck.

The deputy announced with a sweep of his hand, "Ya'll can go now, all except for this one," pointing to Rufus Fripp's truck. "I want to check this one again. Ya'll go on now. Git."

The other drivers cast nervous looks around at each other, as if asking themselves what to do. Cephus Green, number two truck driver in the caravan, spoke up.

"Rufus, dis don' feel right."

"Ya'll do like 'e say now."

Rufus knew this was a no-win situation for his friends. "Do like de Man say. I ketch up wid you d'rectly."

It was an anxious group of farmers who turned their trucks back toward town.

The Hun called Deputy Rollins over to the patrol car. "Go take a piss or something. I need a word with Mr. Fripp."

"Sir?"

"You heard me, boy."

The young deputy had often been instructed to "go take a piss", meaning don't come back until I call you. He didn't want to know.

The Hun got up in Rufus' face. "You goddamned uppity nigger. Who the fuck do you think you are, messing with the Sheriff and his friends? You and that limey bastard, Driftwood, done fucked up for the last time, sickin' the Feds down on us. I know you got some gold still hid away. You gonna tell me where it is, right here and right now." And to make his point, the Hun jammed the butt of his nightstick hard into Rufus' stomach. A lesser man would have gone to his knees, but not Rufus Fripp. Barrel chested, with broad shoulders, and forearms the size of stove pipes, Rufus was not the kind of man to trifle with, lest you had the paper power of the law behind you. A field crate of tomatoes weighs a hundred and twenty pounds. Rufus routinely hefted one on each shoulder.

"You ain't nuttin' but de Sheriff yawd dog. I en't tellin' you nuttin'. The mighty sword of Joshua gwine strike you down for yo sins."

The Hun became a mountain of rage. Off his leash now, he was free to inflict all the suffering his feral brain could divine, aiming a crushing blow of his nightstick to Rufus' head. It never connected. With the strength of forty years working in the fields, Rufus grabbed the stick in his left hand and delivered a mighty right fist to the Hun's snarling face. Glasses shattered, and a smashed nose sprayed bright red blood, the Hun staggered backward against the patrol car. A lifetime of self-deprecating deference to "The Man" unleashed itself in Rufus, following with a hammer left fist to the kidneys, and a right upper cut that sent the Hun's head smashing through the cars side window. The Hun slumped to the ground. The face of corruption and intimidation lay powerless in the sand. "You jes stay down now, like da sorry pile o sheriff shit you is."

With the realization of what had just happened, Rufus knew he had to get gone, and fast. He made three steps towards his truck, grabbed the door handle, when he turned back toward a heaving, sucking sound. Raised to one knee was the Hun, gurgling blood through busted teeth, pistol drawn. A single crack of the Smith & Wesson .38 brought Deputy Rollins running. He found the Hun face down in the sand, pistol hand outstretched before him, and Rufus Fripp slumped on the running board of his truck, shot in the back.

Screaming sirens met the sheriff at the hospital. The Hun was rushed away on a gurney to the emergency room, leaving the young deputy to explain what happened. A black orderly took Rufus away under a sheet to a segregated waiting room. The Sheriff ordered a security blanket of silence on the case until he had a full accounting. He pulled the deputy aside and grilled him on the details.

"Rollins, how did this get so fucked up? And where the hell were you?"

"Sheriff, sir, it was Joe, sheriff. He was way out of line. He started the whole thing."

"Don't you back talk me, boy. Joe was doin' his job. Why weren't you there doin' yours, backing Joe up?"

"I was pissin'."

"Take a few days off. Lay low. Get drunk. I don't care. Just keep your goddamn mouth shut and stay out of sight until I call for you."

Back in the smoke-filled meeting room the Big Men paced in unfamiliar discomfort. Big John sat stoically at the mahogany table where he routinely ordered the pace and fate of other men's lives, with his arms crossed, chewing a half-smoked Havana stogie. He motioned for the Sheriff, who came around the table and leaned down close to his summons.

"Sheriff, I thought you had this situation under control. Now we got no gold, an officer in the hospital, and one gunshot nigger to explain away."

"I got it, I got this."

"You just better not drag me into this mess, you hear me?" Stabbing at the Sheriffs' badge, he made his point. "Everybody thinks that badge of yours runs this county. You and I know better. I pinned that badge on you and I can take it away. I sit behind the curtain and pull the strings. You dance to my tune. Don't you ever forget it. Now, fix this mess!"

A flushed sheriff straightened and retreated to the other side of the table. One of the other Big Men pounded the table with his fist. "Son of a bitch."

The sheriff regained his composure, "Too bad the nigger didn't kill Joe, too. We'd be rid of them both."

"You're one cold mother fucker, Sheriff."

"Loose ends, Judge, loose ends."

The Hun's mouth was wired shut to heal a broken jaw and busted teeth. The deputy was nowhere to be found, and Rufus was nearly dead and unable to speak. The other farmers did not actually see what happened. The sheriff managed to get ahead of the next day's newspaper story about the "Traffic Stop Gone Wrong". According to an official statement from the Sheriff's Department, "One Rufus Fripp was stopped for a broken tail light. It was apparent he had been drinking. When questioned by the Sheriff's Deputy, Mr. Fripp became belligerent and physically assaulted the deputy, who was forced to defend himself. Mr. Fripp was wounded in the scuffle. Charges are pending."

When news of Rufus' shooting reached the Island, a great mourning roused the entire Gullah community. There would be time enough for justice. Driftwood made a solemn vow to that. It was time to bring Rufus home.

The doctors at the hospital pulled the bullet from Rufus' back, but it did little good. There was nerve damage. He had no feeling in his arms and legs. His breathing was shallow and intermittent; pneumonia and respiratory failure was imminent.

For three days and nights friends and family tended Rufus' "sit up". They sang Gullah spirituals and prayed to give Rufus the strength to *"pass death's door, "tuh hep 'em cross de ribber."* On the third day Rufus' eyes opened. He seemed to rally a bit, calling his family about him in a feeble whisper. He called, too, for his longtime friend, Driftwood.

"Mama, don' worry 'bout me. I's soon to be wid' the Lawd. Missa Cory, de Sheriff dog, he try t' git yo secret out me. Me and Joshua d'nt tell'm nuttin. Promise me you take care o' my Jezebel."

Driftwood knelt at his friend's bedside. With tears in his eyes and love in his heart, Driftwood clasped both his hands to Rufus' rough and callused left hand, and swore on all that was holy, "I will take care of them, and make things a'right." He squeezed hard, in hopes of holding the soul of his friend a moment longer. Rufus smiled his infectious smile, and with a final breath, eased on to Glory. Driftwood bowed his head and wept quietly.

With Rufus stilled in death, a slow moan began deep down in his Jezebel's soul. It built as she rocked back and forth over Rufus' body, roaring out in a primal scream of mortal anguish. The "Death Shout" was quickly followed by all in attendance to Rufus' passing. Everyone knew Rufus Fripp "done cross ober". The ritual shouting would keep the spirits of hell from lurking around trying to steal Rufus' soul.

The funeral preparations lasted two days. As was Gullah custom, Rufus' body was washed, and dressed in white sheets before being put into his coffin.

Rufus' funeral service was held behind The First African Baptist Church down by the river on a beautiful Sunday morning. All the congregation was there; the men dressed in black, the women in white. The church choir led beautiful Gullah spirituals during the eulogy and internment. Gathered in a circle about Rufus's coffin the singers broke down the chorus of lyrics into a cadenced ritual, clapping hands and swaying, all singing united, one body, one soul, helping Rufus's soul cross "ober t' de other side":

I know moon rise, I know star rise

Lay dis body down.

I walk in de moonlight, I walk in de star light,

To lay dis body down.

The High Sheriff sent the Hun to watch the funeral service. His presence was intended to be a subtle reminder of the Sheriff's power and reach. Not even the dark sunshades and low brimmed hat could hide the savage beating Rufus laid on him. He would be eating through a straw for months.

> *I'll walk in de graveyard, I'll*
> *walk through de graveyard*
>
> *To lay dis body down.*

Not even the somber tone of the funeral service could keep vengeful eyes of the crowd from glancing toward the patrol car idling nearby. One in particular, who, out of respect for Rufus' family, and by superstition, chose to watch from a distance.

> *I'll lie in de grave and stretch out*
> *my arms,*
>
> *Lay dis body down.*

The Hun had to pee. After all the IV fluids pumped through him the last few days in the hospital, he had to piss every half hour. When he stepped out of his patrol car and behind a large Live Oak tree to relieve himself, Dr. Snake drifted past the car, seen, and unseen, as vague as a wisp of smoke. He was not alone. Dr. Snake called on "de debil's serpent" to do the Lord's work, dropping a large rattlesnake into the driver's window of the patrol car.

As the final song of the service continued, the Hun decides to leave. He had made his point. Besides, his head and face hurt like Billy Hell. He reached under the seat of his patrol car for the medicinal whiskey bottle hidden there. Even through busted teeth he mumbled, "This'll take the edge off."

Instead of a bottle, he grabbed something that grabbed him back. The Hun snatched his hand back from under the seat. It throbbed with pain, and drooled blood from two small holes in the palm of his hand. Eyes wide with sudden recognition, the Hun tried to stomp the rattlesnake writhing about his foot pedals. Hitting the gas peddle hard, the patrol car lunged at full throttle through the funeral congregation, like Moses parting the Red Sea, launching itself fifty feet out over the creek bank and into the soft pluff mud.

The choir never missed a beat.

*I go to de judgement in de evenin'
of de day,*

When I lay dis body down.

The Hun crawled out the window of the mired patrol car and started bogging back toward high ground, clutching his wounded hand. Smelling foul of the dead detritus at the bottom of the tidal marsh, the mud got softer and softer. He bogged down, first to his thighs, then to his waist, his eyes full with fright, the tide was coming in slowly and the more he struggled, the tighter he was imprisoned. He locked eyes with Dr. Snake, rocking from side to side, chanting some gibberish curse. The Hun's orders for help from the crowd quickly turned to pleas. The singing continued. Higher and higher rose the water; to his arm pits, then his shoulders. He began wailing for the mercy he never showed his victims. The muddy water strangled the gurgling sound from his throat as his final thrashings sank from view.

177

And my soul and your soul will
meet in de day,

When I lay dis body down.

The chorus ended with a clapping crescendo. The rising tide erased all trace of the Hun.

The singing crowd closed the service with,

Pharaoh's Army Got Drowned.

Driftwood turned away from the crowd and nodded to Dr. Snake.

"Amen, my friend. Amen"

CHAPTER XXII
Redemption

Driftwood's life changed dramatically after Rufus' death. With his best friend dead and no place to stay, he took a cot in the basement of a local Catholic church in town, in return for doing handiwork. He became a local fixture about town, the kind of character everyone knew by sight, but almost no one talked to" a castaway in plain sight.

Driftwood's feud with the law had cooled. Rufus was dead, the Hun drowned, no more to gain, no more to lose, and "to 'ell with that cursed gold!"

Driftwood's one-real contact with reality was the Irish pastor of the Catholic Church, Father Flannigan. He, too, had kinfolk back in Ireland. They became as close to being friends as Driftwood was capable. Father Flannigan didn't chide Driftwood about the pint always under his cot.

179

And he was there, often unbeknownst to Driftwood, when he went into his hallucinogenic states. This was as close to a demonic possession as Father Flannigan cared to get.

It was during one of Driftwood's nightmare ramblings that Father Flannigan heard something he could not ignore or casually dismiss as the ranting of a tortured soul.

Father Flannigan was awakened at three o'clock one morning by the sound of furniture slamming into walls and what sounded like several people swearing and fighting down in the church basement. He crept down the stairway and into one of Driftwood's nightmares. Driftwood was dancing about as a prize fighter might shadow box the adversary of an upcoming bout, ducking invisible blows, swinging wildly and cursing imaginary foes.

"Donavan, I'm standing here, man, your marble-eyed bastard. Come 'an bust me round top me skull, if ye can. 'An you there, High Sheriff, come an take yer best shot. Old Driftwood's a waitin' fer 'ya. If it's me gold yer wantin' you'll have to come an' get it. What's that you say? 'Angin'. You'll not be takin' me back to England on that score. That sailor had it comin', trying to steal me poke, he was. I downed him right enough. It was a fair fight, sent him to Glory, I did."

Spinning to confront the new adversary, Driftwood grabbed a mesmerized Father Flannigan by his frock, about to thrash him too, when he suddenly snapped back to reality, his mad eyes refocusing mere inches from Father Flannigan's ashen face. With recognition, came a simple question as pure as Sunday communion.

"Father Flannigan, what the duce are you doin' down 'ere at this late hour?"

A stunned Father Flannigan, week in the knees, slumped into a chair. Where he can keep close the confessions of his flock, murder was another thing altogether. He could not let this pass, for his own safety and for the redemption of Driftwood's soul.

The next morning Driftwood carried about as if the previous nights' fit was as any other; nightmares brushed back into the dark recesses of his mind by the new day's sunshine. Not so, for Father Flannigan. He resolved to ferret this out, find the truth. But that was forty years ago, if it actually happened at all.

Father Flannigan knew Driftwood's best friend was Rufus Fripp. Would Driftwood have ever talked about his past? But Rufus was dead. Could Rufus' wife Jezebel know what Rufus may have known? Father Flannigan felt he was walking a fine line. He could not ask Jezebel about the incident outright, without violating his cardinal oath to protect Driftwood's confidence. But if she offered the information to him, well that was a different thing. How to approach Jezebel?

Father Flannigan asked Jonathan, the church janitor, for his help in meeting with Jezebel.

"Tell her it's a matter of saving a man's soul." He was counting on Jezebel's deep faith to help her agree to a meeting.

Following a quiet knock, the sanctuary door opened to a tall black woman, hair white with age, proud, her back ramrod straight. Jezebel addressed Father Flannigan, "What's can I do in service to de Lawd?"

Directing her toward a pew to sit, "Jezebel, thank you for agreeing to meet with me. I have a problem that only you may be able to help me resolve."

"I do what's I can."

"Jezebel, I know Mister Cory and your Rufus were close friends for a long time, and Cory lived with you and Rufus for several years, until he built his own place on Harbor Island."

"Das right."

"Did Cory ever tell Rufus about his past, I mean about where he came from and how he got here?"

"Well, he did talk some 'bout dem early time. But wid Missa Cory it hard tellin' de truth fum he dream talk. Ain't nobody wanna git dat close to de man. Bes I kin tell, he be runnin' fum hard times when he git here. Sometime Missa Cory an' Rufus sit out back de house to de barn affa long days work, sippin some Trip Legree shine. Sometime they be laughin' sometime a cryin'. Dey share de smoke wit Missa Cory pipe. De was real close, my Rufus and Missa Cory.

"You said Cory was running away from something bad. Did Rufus ever tell you what that was?"

"Well, like I say, I neba put no faith in Missa Cory tall tales, an' he Irish speak be hod to unerstan'. But Rufus say Cory be runnin' from de debil fo' knifing a man back up North, place call Norf' Virginia. Rufus say Cory jus' come 'er fum de war. Dat de Fall 'o 1916, when Rufus bring Missa Cory to de island. It Missa Cory soul need savin'? My Rufus babtize Mr. Cory in de ribber he sef."

"All our souls need help from time to time. Thank you, Mrs. Fripp, for taking the time to meet with me. Jonathan will drive you home."

"An you have a bless day, Reverend."

Father Flannigan collected his thoughts. *So, Cory was an Irish war veteran. The Irish conscripts fought for the British Army. There must be records at the British War Office. I need help putting this together.*

The young banker, sent to Federal prison for his father's money laundering crimes, earned an early release from prison. He came home to learn that Driftwood was living in the basement of the Catholic Church, his church. Barred from banking for life, he set about managing the family's considerable real estate holdings. The young banker was of a different time than that of his father. He had been sent off to boarding school at age eight and went to college out of state. His was a new world view. Having grown up watching the business dealings of his father and the other Big Men, the young banker vowed to try to make things right, as best he could, a little generational guilt tugging at his heart. His wealth and community status were largely built from the secret gold vault beneath his daddy's bank. He owed Driftwood better than the hand life had dealt him. He went to see Father Flannigan about the matter.

"It's a good thing you stopped by to ask about Cory. But there is a more immediate issue I need your help with.

"Yes, Father, what do you need?"

Father Flannigan laid it all out.

Together Father Flannigan and the banker wired an inquiry to the Office for Veterans Affairs in England.

"Yes, there is a record of a private Ian Hugh Cory, of the Tyneside Irish Brigade, serving with a forward regiment on the Somme in the fall of 1916. He is listed MIA, missing in action by a First lieutenant Beaumont. Sorry, but there is nothing more."

Disheartened, Father Flannigan was lost about how to proceed.

The banker brought focus to the question. "Father Flannigan, we have Cory in the service, in the Battle of the Somme, and somehow later showing up in Norfolk, Virginia, in a bar fight. Pack some traveling clothes, we're going to Norfolk."

The county library in Norfolk maintained newspaper reports going all the way back to the town's original founding. The fall of 1916 was only twelve weeks of the last forty years. It took three days and gallons of hot coffee to read every story of those twelve weeks, but they found it:

A row last night at O' Reilly's pub put one man, a British sailor named Brian Cotsworth, in the hospital with a gashing belly wound from a broken beer bottle. His chances of recovery at this writing appear positive. Mr. Cotsworth has been charged with drunk and disorderly conduct and disturbing the peace. His fine is pending his discharge from Norfolk General Hospital, after which he will be placed aboard the next coaling ship to England. Mr. Cotsworth assailant's identity is unclear, although he is described as a wiry Irishman with one blue and one brown eye. Authorities have not been unable to locate this man, but corroborating testimony from many patrons in the bar that night support a claim of self-defense. There are no charges pending against this queer eyed mystery man.

About to put the newspaper away, the banker noticed a hand-written note in the margin. "Copied by request of Beaufort County Sheriff's Department, August 11, 1938."

His conscience cleared of any doubts, Father Flannigan and the banker headed for home. The High Sheriff had known the truth all along. He was bluffing.

Driftwood's life took an upbeat path, one somewhat mellowed by life's toll on his 70 odd years. His deep-seated angers largely spent, and haunting demons held at bay with a steady supply of rum, allowed a long-repressed Hugh Cory to molt into an almost normal human being, his transition like the seventeen-year cicada emerging from its long dark sleep. His mood was lighter, his eyes sharp and quick, his step a little crisper.

The young banker gave Driftwood rent free use of a small one room cottage down by the river off Bay Street, and a monthly stipend for food, tobacco, and a medicinal supply of rum. He even had a local shrimper tow Driftwood's bateau from Horseshoe Point to the downtown waterfront so the old man could stay close to his river lifestyle. The family bank stock was worth millions; it was the least he could do. The cottage even had modern plumbing.

With the banker's patronage, Driftwood was no longer the pariah he had once been. He took odd jobs repairing furniture about town and making deliveries for Ma Millers grocery store in return for the occasional dip into the beer cooler. Gullah spiritual face carvings appeared on several palmetto trees about town. Driftwood continued to make palmetto masks and totems for those favored few allowed passage into Driftwood's "inner place".

Driftwood developed a following of sorts, amongst young boys around town, despite their parent's protests. The boys admired his carefree lifestyle, unhampered by the rules and moors of conventional society. Driftwood made his own rules, seemingly to mock everything normal. The Somme had torn away one reality, so Driftwood made up another, an alternative universe where he was the grand puppet master. Sigmund and Albert would have been impressed.

One such lad indulged Driftwood with the patience of Job and was rewarded with a daily dose of lusty jokes and wistful imaginings that would later be relegated to the memories of misspent youth. But for the time, they were the tales that let his young mind piggyback Driftwood's eccentric ramblings.

On one warm Saturday morning the young boy arrived at Driftwood's place for a promised fishing trip. He waited, and waited, and waited some more. Forty-five minutes passed and still no Driftwood. The impatient lad began a bored fumbling about with some of Driftwood's things in the small building, smelling an empty rum bottle and quickly pushing it aside. "Ugh, how can he drink this stuff?" A carving knife with its fluted cutting edge came to hand, then a half-finished palmetto mask. Beneath a window facing the river was a weathered old writing desk Driftwood had scavenged from a local trash bin and restored. Unique in its orderly arrangement of books, writing paper, pen, and spectacles, it stood an island alone in a sea of chaos. Pushing it out of mind, the boy turned to leave when a startling "HEY" shouted from above. Driftwood dropped from the low hanging rafters, nearly causing the boy to wet himself. He had been hiding up there, spider like, waiting "To see if you'd be a stealin' me polk." But then, like turning off a mood switch, "Let's go fishing, lad. Grab us a couple 'o them cans off the shelf for lunch."

"Mister Cory, there's no labels on 'em. How do you know what they are?"

The local Piggly Wiggly grocery store gave Driftwood the dented and damaged produce cans they couldn't put on the shelves, in return for occasional maintenance work.

"Don't know, lad, don't care. Can't ya se? That's the fun of it, a mystery surprise in every one."

The re-born Driftwood had lightened life's load from his shoulders somewhat. But behind those questioning blue and brown eyes still lay an uneasy truce with reality. Where most people socially and intuitively respected a neutral space between one another of about eighteen inches, Driftwood routinely pressed that by half, touching, pulling in exaggerated mannerisms, getting so close one could almost see into the tortured soul behind those offset blue and brown eyes. Even to those few befriended by Driftwood, there was the unmistakable feeling that this was a man teetering on the edge of self-control, with but the lightest jostling needed to set him off.

The fishing trip was unlike any other the young boy had been on, or ever would be again. A newly constructed center pivot swing bridge had been built connecting downtown Beaufort to the outer islands. The old bridge had been dismantled, all but the concrete foundations. That day they were to be dynamited to clear the waterway.

Driftwood and the boy rowed the bateau underneath the waterfront wharves watching the demolition crews set their charges. Lunch was one can of mystery peaches, the other, beans and franks. The warning sirens, signaling a pending blast, were quickly followed by a loud "whoomph" and then by concrete crashing into a boiling hole in the water.

"Quick now, lad, lean to your oar."

Matching the old man stroke for stroke, the two darted from beneath their hiding place to collect a dozen stunned Sheepshead and Red Drum fish in a scoop net. Overhead the blasting crew hollered and cussed.

"Out of the way, old man. You're gonna get yourself killed."

Driftwood turned a deaf ear, and pulling aboard the last fish, gave the lad a nod to retreat to the wharf.

Three sirens, three blasts, and three times the bateau rushed to gather a bounty of fish. Three times the blast crew hurled down their curses and warnings to deaf ears. When Driftwood heard police sirens approaching the bridge, he gave the "heave to" to his mate and off they made, fast as they could row, under the full length of the city wharves to the other end of town.

Safely away, Driftwood and the boy loaded the fish into a hand cart Driftwood had positioned earlier for the job of hauling his catch to the fish market, two city blocks away. Thirty dollars in hand, Driftwood slapped the young boy on the shoulder, and peeled off a $5-dollar bill.

"Well done, lad. Now off with you. I've an appointment with me Cuban delusion," he said, nodding to the Red Dot liquor store down the street.

Ah, but for the women. No one could best an Irishman for tales of conquest. While mostly a legend in his own mind in that regard, outwardly Driftwood loved to flirt with store clerks, women he passed on the street, and especially the young eighteen-year-old secretary for his benefactor, the young banker. When most brushed him off as an eccentric old drunk, the secretary humored the old gentleman with small talk and a cup of coffee when he came around for his monthly stipend. Not a handout, but more honorably a cash purchase of a driftwood carving.

These "works of art", being really quite well done, made unique personal gifts for the banker's friends and customers. The arrangement worked out well for all concerned.

To the surprise of the secretary, several days following her wedding announcement, she found in the banker's office a double-sided, two-faced palmetto totem pole carving, gift wrapped with a small note addressed to her.

189

Undreamt dreams long gone cold

Faded now for those grown old

A young girl's love without repent

A young man's soul mate heaven sent

Both blessed ye now of Driftwood's gold

Enclosed was a single, mint perfect, Spanish gold doubloon.

Late into a summer's eve Driftwood could often be found holding court at his favorite riverfront bar, regaling his audience with a tireless retelling of old tales of Ireland, his grandly imagined romantic conquests, and often hints of golden treasures. Sporting a full head of white hair, a crazy white beard, and missing a few teeth he looked the part of an "old salt".

"Hey, you old coot," hollered out a regular patron, "Tell us the one about the ballerina."

Driftwood climbed atop of the bar, casting his gloriously drunk two-toned eyes about the crowd, entreating every man there to "Grab a'holt o' yerself there mate and pour old Driftwood another round. The ballerina it is then.

"A large woman, quite fetching she was, and wearing a sleeveless sundress, walked into me pub one night. She raised her right arm, revealing a huge, hairy armpit, and pointed to all me friends sitting around the pub to ask, 'What lad here will buy a woman a drink?' The pub went silent, dead quiet as St. John's ghost. Every man jack one of 'em tried to ignore her. Down at the far end of the bar sat an owl-eyed drunk. 'E slammed 'is hand down on the counter and bellowed, 'Give the ballerina a drink'. The bartender poured the drink, and a stiff one at that. Well now, the woman chugged it down in one mighty swaller." Driftwood animated his soliloquy in a single gulp of Irish rye whiskey.

"She turned to me friends, and pointed 'round once more, revealing the same hairy armpit, and asked, 'What good lad will buy a lady another drink?' Once again, the little drunk at the end of the bar slammed 'is money down on the bar saying, 'Give the ballerina another drink!'

"The bartender, now quite perplexed, approached the little drunk and asked, 'Tell me, Paddy, it's yer own business to be buyin' the lady a drink. But, why do you keep calling her the ballerina?' Paddy replied, 'Any woman who can lift her leg that high has to be a ballerina.'"

The bar roared tears of laughter at Driftwood's final soliloquy of the night.

The bartender slid Driftwood a rum "roady" to go, and a nod of thanks for another full house, come to hear his colorful renditions.

Walking out into the cooler night air, the pungent, salty smell of the river pluff mud at low tide offered its sobering poultice to over indulgence. Driftwood pulled his pipe from his shirt pocket, lighting it for a long satisfying pull of strong tobacco. Three strangers followed Driftwood and his stories of pirate gold out into the night. Confident of an easy mark, they quietly caught up to the old man in a side alley and under cover of his whistling tunes, slammed him to the ground from behind, cursing and kicking the downed man.

"Where you got that gold hid, you barnacled son of a bitch. You tell us now, or we gonna' bust you up good."

Irish blood, heated by pain and numbed by alcohol, was a dangerous brew. Driftwood's arms, flailing to ward off the blows, chanced upon a three-foot piece of two-by-four scrap lumber lying on the ground next to the trash bin he was pinned against. Searing pain and boiling anger found their moment. The three assailants were no longer pounding an old, helpless bum, but the distant sired son of Cu Chulainn, Irish hero and warrior king.

Rolling to one knee, Driftwood's first blow took out the legs of the nearest mugger. On his feet now, the cudgel in his hands went to work backing his attackers into the very alley they had thrown him, their trap now became his killing field. A shattered forearm here, busted skull there, and a couple of broken ribs quickly turn the mugging into a drubbing.

Driftwood, confident of the quality of his defense, turned to leave when a bullet, fired from the fallen hand of a last breath boot pistol, struck him squarely in the back. When he dropped the bloodied lumber to the ground all went quiet in the alley, save for a few low, painful moans.

The Druid Kings of legend would have been proud. With the rush of adrenalin subsiding, the exhausted Driftwood leaned against the alley wall and pulled his tin half-pint from his back pocket; wiped his left shirtsleeve across his nose to staunch the bloody flow from his ruptured lungs and took a hit of rum. He turned to survey the last few moments work with an odd half smile, and hocked up a twisted .38 caliber slug, spitting it dismissively onto the dead face of his vanquished assailant. As Driftwood stepped from the alley back into the street, a coward's blow felled him from behind. An unseen fourth man, sent to make sure of the work of the first three, slid away into the night. Neville's pipe lay crushed beneath his boot.

The gunshot emptied the bar into the street.

The mystery attack sent Driftwood to the hospital emergency room. There were rumors that this was a vendetta mugging, but no one was arrested. The head trauma and gunshot damage he suffered in the mugging were irreversible. In and out of consciousness, Driftwood babbled deliriously about his treasure, calling himself "Ben Gun".

"Ben Gunn knows. Old Ben knows." His eyes widened as he rose up on one elbow staring out into space, addressing an audience only he could see. In a rasping laugh, he muttered a repeated limerick.

> *"Fearful finding, frightful hold,*
> *Three-fold chests of dead men's souls,*
> *Buried deep, forgotten long,*
> *Yellow gleams its siren song,*
> *Of Old Ben's secret, never told"*

Father Flannigan arrived in time to give Driftwood last rights. With his last breath, Driftwood reached out for his lost mates across the great divide.

"T-Tom, Neville, let's up an' away, lads."

He died alone in a room full of strangers. His only personal affects, besides his ratty old clothes, were his whiskey flask, slave dime necklace, a tattered copy of *Treasure Island*, and one of the horseshoe crab masks he was noted for making at his roadside shack on Harbor Island. In his jacket pocket was a faded military shoulder patch.

No one from the Sheriff's Department ever asked about the attack. There was no family to claim the body so Father Flannigan and the banker's son make the arrangements. Ian Hugh "Driftwood" Cory was quietly interred in the county graveyard, with little fanfare. Only days later did news of the murder reach the islands. Rufus' daughter came to pay her respects and read over Driftwood with a passage from her daddy's Bible. In it she found a yellowed letter and instructions. Thereafter, under cover of darkness, an occasional Gullah talisman or trinket appeared on the gravesite. The black grounds keepers were careful not to disturb them.

Shortly after Driftwood's funeral, two letters simultaneously reached their destinations; they were the copies of the letter found in Rufus' bible. One was sent to the Department of Veterans Affairs in Ireland, and the other addressed to the local newspaper.

The letter to Ireland answered many questions. The last unclaimed member of the Tyneside Irish Brigade had been found. The decades-old mystery of who had been sending money to build a memorial to the fallen was solved; it was time for long-lost Ian Hugh Cory to go home.

One week later a representative of The Irish Repatriation Task Force, charged with repatriating the remains of Irish veterans of both World Wars, came to town. He had diplomatic papers, from both the United States government and Ireland, authorizing the re-internment of Private Cory to his home country.

The same day a huge story broke on the front page of the local newspaper. The Sheriff's Department was inundated with reporters.

"Goddamn that sorry limey bastard. Irish Repatriation Force, my ass," bellowed the stammering Sheriff.

Driftwood's story set off a gold rush. Holes were dug all over the islands, in Rufus' fields, at Driftwood's old shack site, as well as his grave site. Rumors flew about the political corruption that built the town. Staid families readied themselves for the aftershock. All the while, the map on the wall at the Johnson Creek Tavern held the answer, mum to a secret in plain sight.

When the scandal unfolded, the High Sheriff was forced to resign. The Judge was removed from the bench, the City Attorney disbarred, and the mayor retired for "health reasons". The Big Boss' radio station went mercifully quiet. The powerful grip of the Big Men was finally broken. Big Law had come to town.

A newly-constructed high span bridge several miles upriver connecting the islands to town, originally to be named after the High Sheriff, was renamed for Driftwood's contribution to the economic recovery of post-Recession Beaufort. The ceremony was a mix of town folk and Gullah farmers. Presiding over the affair was the Big Banker's son, his reputation restored in the title of the new Mayor-elect. Newly-appointed Sheriff Thad Rollins' announced his hiring of a black deputy to patrol the islands and restore the lost trust so often trampled upon by the last administration. The ceremonial cutting of the ribbon attended the new Bank Manager's proclamation that Driftwood's gold, continually compounded and re-invested over those many years, had a hundred-million-dollar impact on Beaufort's rebirth.

In the half century following the bloody knife fight with Donovan, Cory had survived "The War to end all Wars", made peace with his demons, and purged the pirates' blood money. He earned the respect of a foreign culture, exposed a corrupt political system, and was returning home a war hero.

When asked about a new name for the bridge, Rufus' wife Jezebel answered, "We's all in dis t'gether. Missa Cory, 'e come 'ere a troubled man runnin' from e Debil, an' 'e gone to Glory by de grace o' Gawd. Call it Redemption Crossing".

CHAPTER XXIII
Gone Home

The wind picked up from the south, bringing the heavy sweet smell of rain. Another storm was coming to the islands.

The stone cutter in Ireland just finished the last inscription on the memorial to the fighting men of the 34th Irish Brigade. Two thousand miles across the Atlantic, the exhumed remains of Private Ian Hugh Cory were piped aboard a jet plane bound for Ireland. It was a happy tune, played on traditional Irish pipes.

The plane took off from the Lady's Island airport ahead of the approaching storm and the sound of rolling thunder. Down below on Harbor Island, dust devils danced across the sandy footprints of a long-gone shack. A gaunt old man in dark clothes, straw hat and shades, gently buried a small blue amulet in a burned-out doorway,

197

cocking his ear to a distant Gullah melody whistling through the bowed palmettos.

Swing Low, Sweet Chariot. Driftwood
Cory has gone home.

Amen!

Epilogue:

In the years since Driftwood's passing, a fish camp was built on the palmetto island behind Horseshoe Point. Storms and erosion wrought many changes to the island. The large salt cedar trees of Driftwood's time long dead, no more than relic stumps on a hard pan marsh.

Summertime saw regular camp use by the families that built it. Their children swam the creeks, cast for shrimp, fished, and crabbed. The cool, nighttime breeze in the palmettos lulled many a tired child to his bunk, with dreams of adventure, ghosts, and pirate tales. An old horseshoe crab mask watched over them from one corner of the room.

A young boy, hunting fiddler crabs for fish bait out behind the camp, chased some big ones under an old cedar tree stump. He started after them with his shovel when it hit something with a dull "thunk".

It wasn't fiddler crabs that fell from his shovel.

"Daddy, Daddy, look what I found!" said the boy excitedly.

The father was expecting to see an old whiskey bottle or empty gun shell. He reeled in shock at the object in the boy's hands. He took it, turning it to the sun with shaking disbelief. On his knees, elbow deep under the stump, he pulled out a handful of fate from a rotted canvas bag; eyes wide open, his hands trembled with the aspirations of the newly infected.

"Daddy…?"

GIBBES McDOWELL

Yellow glows its siren song...

"Driftwood" Corry
Courtesy Beaufort District Collection
Beaufort County Library, Beaufort, SC

GIBBES McDOWELL

AUTHOR'S POSTSCRIPT:
Channeling Driftwood

Writing "Driftwood Unmasked" took me four years to build a fictitious story around the almost fictitious, colorful character everyone in 1960's and 70's Beaufort, South Carolina called "Driftwood". Thirty-five-years dead and the lack of any proven information about the man gave me a clean canvas on which to paint my story.

Driftwood had it all. He was, by all accounts, unconventional in lifestyle and mannerism, to the extreme. Wild Irish to the bone, he lived the life we saw from the outside by his own rules. Such brash individualism stood in stark contrast to the social norms and conventions of the times. The rest of us were expected to live our lives inside a prescribed set of rules, but Driftwood suffered no such shackles.

Truth is truly a fickle mistress, assumption and prejudice but mirages, showing us only what we expect to see. So, it is with people who don't square with "normal". Beaufort's Driftwood Cory was such a character.

Being an only son, I, too, ran my own race, shunning the "me too" crowd. I won some and lost some. We all have our own baggage to carry, our own destiny to fulfill. That being said, I admit to vesting some of my loner personality traits into my Driftwood character, a kindred spirit, if you will. My fictional Driftwood mirrors some of my own perceptions and world view mirages. I swear on my Daddy's bones; post manuscript revelations of Driftwood's story did not bleed backwards into the already-finished piece.

During the writing of "Driftwood Unmasked" I made every effort to find the real Cory. Even among those closest to him, from whom I borrowed anecdotal stories about Driftwood or who had one of his palmetto face or driftwood carvings, none knew his real name beyond Hugh. One thought he recalled the name Patrick. All thought his last name was spelled Cory or Corey. Nothing could be found of Driftwood in local records, city and county census files, military service records, utility companies, or coroner files. The man was real in body, but invisible otherwise. No one could recollect exactly how or when Driftwood came to Beaufort, or when he disappeared. He was a colorful mystery man with no name or known history. It was rumored that he was AWOL from the British Navy or maybe an on-the-run Irish Republican Army vigilante. Nothing but rumors, twenty years here, wild, crazy, outrageous, artful, humorous, and witty. Then he was gone.

"Driftwood Unmasked" was in final re-write and finished to my mind, when out of the blue I ran into an old Beaufort native, come home for the weekend. Pam Koth, daughter of J.M. Koth of the real Koth's Grocery at the corners of Bladen and North streets, catty-cornered to the Federal Courthouse on Bay Street. She mentioned she heard I was writing a story about Driftwood. Pam volunteered that she knew Driftwood from her teenage years and Driftwood had given her a pair of gold earrings from a deceased wife. Another longtime Beaufort resident told me he remembered "Cory's wife to be a petit blond Cory called 'Miss Baby', living with Cory on Harbor Island in the early 1960's, in his driftwood festooned shack. They were a close couple, living a simple life collecting and crafting driftwood and odd bits that washed up on the beach."

Both echoed the same appraisal of Driftwood that everyone I interviewed shared. "Driftwood was witty, articulate, a little edgy, but altogether the most unique person I ever met."

The unexpected key to opening Driftwood's past came when Pam Koth told me she had a book Driftwood had given to her father. According to Pam, her dad was as close to being a friend of Driftwood as anyone was allowed to get. J. M. Koth let Driftwood hang around the store, swapping cleaning chores for free beer and boiled peanuts, a fair trade all 'round. As I would later discover, J. M. and Driftwood both served in the U. S. Navy during World War II. There was a common bond.

The book Pam Koth found in her father's attic, "The 50 Most Influential Lives of the Twentieth Century", had written inside the dust cover the name of the book's owner, H. P. Knox Corry. I took a deep breath. A name at last! It was a name that jived with the tidbits I had collected. The 'H' corroborated the name Hugh. The 'P' a possible Patrick. And where does Knox fit in? The last name Corry was the closer. How many Hugh Patrick Knox Corrys can there be with a handle like that? Who would have guessed a river bum like Driftwood was reading the likes of "The 50 Most Influential Lives of the Twentieth Century"? With a real name I renewed my search for the real Driftwood Cory.

The exemplary staff at the Beaufort District Collection, upstairs in the Beaufort Library, helped me unearth a gold mine of information. The finding was surreal, the life of Hugh Patrick Knox Corry was an uncanny parallel to the total fiction I had begun writing four years earlier. The twists and turns of my imaginary Driftwood Cory seemingly channeled the life of one of Beaufort's most colorful characters.

Here is the brief story of the real Driftwood Cory, my attempt to restore a little dignity to a man most assumed had none. In thanks for the journey he led me on these last few years, I owe him no less:

We knew Driftwood was Irish. We also knew he was already an old man by the time he disappeared from Beaufort in the middle 70's. Deducing an age of 70'ish would have placed his birth date in the early 1900's. When Miss Grace, at the Beaufort District Collection entered Driftwood's full name into the search engine Ancestory.Com, and pressed "process" we all crossed our fingers and waited for the screen to come to life. What we found were trail markers, sign posts to Corry's past. Following her intuitive hunches navigating various sites, we found a singular Hugh Corry, a Catholic, painter by trade, married to an Elizabeth Knox, and living at number

47 Joy Street in Belfast Ireland. To them was born on January 21, 1909, one Hugh Patrick Knox Corry, confirmed by a 1911 census, aged two at the time the census was taken. He had a sister age one. There would later be two younger brothers, James and Edward. That same census showed three boarders living with the Corry family, including a cousin Cornelius Knox, laborer, and Agnes Smythe, seamstress. The home was part of three connected buildings at the same address, one being a barber shop, likely the neighborhood hub of social and political discourse.

Now we had a sure hit on Hugh, on Patrick. We answered the question of Knox, and corroborated the last name spelling of Corry. The Corry home was located in the Parish of Shankill, noted stronghold of Irish Republican sentiment, another tie to the rumor that Corry he had been a radical hothead in his youth. The birth date of January 21, 1909, the Joy Street address, and mother's maiden name of Knox consistently followed all subsequent research.

Next, we found Hugh Corry, aged 18, leaving the port of Liverpool, England aboard the steamship *Celtic*, of the White Star line, bound for Boston, USA on the fourth of June, 1927. He listed his occupation on the ship's registry as painter, already known to be the son of a painter. This is noteworthy because one of his odd jobs in Beaufort was as a painter. Additionally, a collection of photographs by Lucille Hassel Culp, taken in and around Beaufort in the 1950s and 1960s, and subsequently donated to the Beaufort District Collection, included a photograph of Driftwood's shack on Harbor Island. Lucille Hassel Culp interviewed Driftwood at the time of the picture, adding his resume in the margin of her photo, "Painter, raconteur, and beer drinker."

Why would a healthy 18-year-old leave his native home behind? Was he escaping poverty, seeking a better life, or running from the law?

Roger Pinckney XI, native Beaufort son and accomplished author of numerous novels threading fiction through truth in stories about the Lowcountry, including "The Right Side of the River", "Refer Moon", and his latest, "The Mullet Manifesto", knew Driftwood personally. Roger threw a wide loop in his youth. The teenage Roger was known to pull a cork or two, and occasionally shared a bottle with Driftwood. Whether idle whiskey talk or well-oiled tongue, Roger claims that Driftwood told him of a wilder youth back in Ireland, stories of the 1916 Easter Rebellion, "Aye sonny, it was a sad time, the women a crying for the boys who died. But I made it pretty hot for them, me and that long barreled Luger in that pile of bricks." Driftwood's artful soliloquy on the subject ended with his narrowly missing out on a British Navy yard arm hanging that claimed the life of one of his confederates when he boarded a ship for America under an alias. Does this story have real ties to Driftwood's childhood in Shankill Parish? Truth or rumor, the man was indeed colorful.

A 1928 Petition for Citizenship in the United States reaffirmed Corry's birth date of January, 21, 1909 in Belfast Ireland, his occupation: salesman. In the petition, Corry declared, "I am not an anarchist, I am not a polygamist, nor a believer in the practice of polygamy." His description was white, standing 5 feet 6 inches tall, weighing 140 pounds, with brown hair and blue eyes. The height matches the Corry later known in Beaufort, as do his ""'sparkling bright blue eyes". The photograph taken with the petition for citizenship mirrors a later 1945 photo of Corry in his Navy dress. Fifty years of hard living may have turned the dark hair white by the time Corry got to

Beaufort, but life never dulled the fire in those fierce blue eyes.

Driftwood did not stay long in America before returning to Ireland.

Was he homesick? Was it family business? Or was it to participate in the brewing political unrest consuming Belfast at the time, as has been rumored? Did the granting of American citizenship provide Corry a shield against arrest by Scotland Yard if he was found out? I can find no official record for the next five missing years.

We then found record of young Driftwood on a second voyage to America, aboard the steamer *Transylvania* on June 26, 1933, listing his occupation as a journalist. Already a painter, and salesman, the young journalist, destined to make his mark on Beaufort, owned and read sophisticated works such as "The 50 Most Influential Lives of the 20th Century", the book he would later give to J.M. Koth. His ribald jokes and bawdy tales of romantic conquests hinted at a well-read past.

Arriving in New York, Hugh Corry took a job as an elevator operator in Chicago at the Blackstone Hotel. A copy of his job application confirms his social security number of 565-01-1696, his home town as Belfast, Ireland, and his mother as Elizabeth Knox.

Again, the next few years are missing. Invisibility became a pattern in Driftwood's life.

At some point, later confirmed in his service records, Corry moved to Santa Monica, California.

At the outbreak of World War Two, Corry's youngest brother Edward was killed fighting in the British Royal Air Force. In 1941 Hugh Corry's other brother, James, was reported killed on Christmas Eve in action against the Germans, while serving in the British Submarine Service.

While I could find no record of Corry's employment history in California, his brothers' deaths could have been the event that triggered his decision to go to war: revenge.

A search of US military records revealed thirty-four-year-old Hugh Patrick Knox Corry's application for enlistment, dated February 6, 1942, just five weeks after James' loss. Following lesser training assignments, and with average fitness reports, save one appearance before the Captains' Mast for fighting, a ship's muster roll shows Corry assigned to the destroyer USS *Bailey*, number DD 492 on May 17, 1942. His military ID # was 412 50 49, his rank Seaman 1c, and later Seaman 1c CM (carpenters mate).

Finding Corry's service history lends credence to some of the wild stories he was known to have shared with young boys in Beaufort, who would sneak away for a few hours, against their parents' protests, to listen to the siren song of wild Irish tales.

The unfounded rumor that Driftwood was AWOL from the British Navy was the root of the military plots and twists in, "Driftwood Unmasked". How else to explain how an itinerate Irishman could become exposed to Polynesian art, and find his penchant for palmetto face carvings, without a history of some time spent in the South Pacific? My fictional history of a real character is amazingly close to the history found after the story was finished; wrong war but similar outcomes.

The arrival of complete U. S. Naval Service Records for Hugh Patrick Knox Corry from the National Personnel Service Center was the lynchpin that brought this story full circle. The application for enlistment confirmed an estranged wife named Katherine Corry living in New York. Her consent form for Corry's enlistment stated that they had no children. His occupation was listed as a carpenter, cabinet maker, and interior decorator. His educational history consisted of eight years of grammar school, four years of high school, and two years of college. Corry was an educated man! The medical exam showed him to be a "scrapper", as evidenced by scars above his left eye, the bridge of his once-broken nose, and on his right knee. He had once been treated for a venereal disease, and had several times been arrested for public drunkenness. His religious affiliation changed from Catholic to Protestant. He failed the night vision Radium Plaque Adaptometer test, meaning he would serve no night time watch duty. Corry bought a serviceman's life insurance policy, payable to Katherine Corry.

The combat history of the destroyer *Bailey* DD 492 is legendary in U. S Naval archives. The Bailey earned a Naval Unit Commendation and nine battle stars. Seaman 1c Hugh Patrick Knox Corry is part of that story. The *Bailey* participated in nearly every major campaign in the Pacific war against the Japanese and in the Aleutian Islands. The Battle of the Komandorski Islands earned the *Bailey* a Naval Unit Commendation by order of the President of the United States to the Secretary of the Navy.

The Japanese Navy had secured several islands in the Aleutian chain of islands, off the extreme east coast of Alaska, giving them a tactical launch point to attack the west coast of America. Keeping those Komandorski Islands bases supplied was critical to the Japanese war effort.

Appositionally true was the American need to uproot the bases and deprive them of re-supply. Driftwood's destroyer, *Bailey* DD-492, was the critical element in defeating the Japanese re-supply effort as detailed in the following letter of commendation.

"Outstanding heroism in action against enemy Japanese forces off Komandorski Islands, Bearing Sea, on March 26, 1943. With the only heavy cruiser of our small task force dead in the water following a fierce three-and-one-half-hour battle, the U.S.S *Bailey* led a determined torpedo attack against the superior Japanese surface force, which was still closing on our ships. Unprotected by friendly aircraft and without benefit of darkness or a smoke screen, she steamed forward at maximum speed, leading two other destroyers through a heavy barrage of hostile gunfire and concentrating her fire on the enemy's leading heavy cruiser. Struck in rapid succession by two 8-inch shells and damaged by numerous near hits as she closed to within 9,000 yards, she launched five torpedoes and turned to retire just before two additional shell hits flooded her and rendered one engine inoperative. The only destroyer to release her torpedoes, the Bailey succeeded in damaging one heavy cruiser and in turning back an overwhelming enemy force at the most crucial point of the battle. Her meritorious record of achievement is evidence of her own readiness for combat and the gallantry and seamanship of her officers and men."

As our Hugh Corry is not here to speak for himself, I have taken several quotes from the memoirs of Officer Stan Hogshead of the *Bailey* about this engagement:

"The captain announced to all hands that this was not just a general quarter's drill, but that we were undoubtedly headed into a battle with a superior enemy force. Battle lines were drawn and speed increased to 25 knots. Soon it was announced that the enemy consisted of two heavy cruisers, two light cruisers, and six destroyers.

We were going to be outgunned almost two to one! You don't expect to survive from odds like that.

"As the word of the torpedo attack was announced to all hands, there was absolute, total silence as we stared at each other and wondered if we could possibly survive it. I didn't and I don't think anyone else did either. We all shook hands and said the words men say when they know they are going to die.

"Speed was increased to 35 knots. We began firing at a range of 12,000 yards getting off a salvo from our two 5-inch bow guns at the rate of one round every twelve seconds. We could hear enemy shells 'kerchunking' into the sea on both sides of us, then came a large explosion just forward of fire control, and another just aft. We began taking on water. Ice cold water was soon up to my knees. I knew my time had come. The *Bailey* held her course, pounding away with all she had. We had closed to 9,500 yards preparing to launch our torpedoes, practically point-blank range for the 8-inch guns of the enemy heavy cruiser.

"Torpedoes away. One confirmed hit.

"As the *Bailey* turned away from its torpedo run it took two more 8-inch rounds to the stern. It was later seen that at least two more cannon rounds had struck the *Bailey* at critical areas, sure to sink the ship-but they bounced off never exploding.

"Five men were killed in the battle, six more wounded. We limped back to Dutch Harbor 1,200 miles away at the speed of 12 knots, our gunnels barely above the waterline, ever ready for the enemy to find us and finish us off."

Seaman Corry's duties as carpenter's mate would have placed him below deck in the bowels of the *Bailey* during this battle, blind to his fate, bound by duty to work through the terror of deafening cannon fire above and the steady pounding of enemy fire all around the boat. After the *Bailey* suffered several near-mortal blows, Corry would have been part of the work crew stuffing and patching the hull against the inrushing seawater, up to his chest in the frigid wash, fighting for the lives of the crew and the *Bailey*. With one engine dead, lights flickering in the darkness, the smell of pending death was in their nostrils. Imagine what that would have been like, the adrenalin rush, the shouts and screams of desperate men. There is no second place in a battle such as that.

The *Bailey*'s tactics in the battle of The Kormandorski Islands is later simulated in naval combat schools where, in each simulation, she fails to survive; just goes to show how guts and determination can win the day against overwhelming odds.

On October 1, 1944 the *Bailey* suffered a midnight strafing while on picket duty off the island of Pelelui. Nine men were killed and sixteen wounded.

After nearly two years of steady combat aboard the *Bailey*, Seaman Corry was transferred to the *Baxter*, a landing support craft, for the last campaigns of the war.

On April 9, 1945 Seaman Corry requested assignment to shore duty as follows:

> Hugh P. K. Corry, above named, respectfully makes request of the Bureau of Naval Personnel, or other appropriate officer, for assignment to shore duty upon the following statement of facts:

> My legal residence is Santa Monica, California. My address was 913 Wilshire Boulevard.

I joined the Navy in 1942 at San Pedro, Calif., taking a physical examination in Los Angeles.

After about three months of duty on board U.S.S *Radio*, about six weeks training in San Diego and about five months at Moffett Field near Pal Alto, Calif., I was assigned to duty on the U.S.S *Bailey*, DD-492. For two years I was on the *Bailey*, which was attached to the 2nd Division of Marines, and of the two years was in about fifteen months of continual combat in the Pacific Ocean. I was in the battles at Tarawa, Kwajalein, Saipan, Tinian, etc. My service bar has four bronze stars and I have a citation bar with a blue star.

Last autumn I was sent home to recover from battle fatigue and on September 29, 1944 reported to the Naval Training Center at Miami, Florida. I am now assigned to PGM-28 for duty in a Pacific command. While at Miami I worked in the repair department. Part of the time I was in the hospital with a broken ankle.

I am the sole support of my parents, Mr. and Mrs. Hugh Corry, of 47 Joy Street, Belfast, Northern Ireland. I am their only son living. My brother Edward was killed while serving in the British Royal Air Force and my brother James was lost at sea in a submarine of the British Navy. My parents were supposed to get $50 per month from the U.S. Government through an allotment of a part of my pay, but of late have been receiving only $37 per month according to a letter from my Mother, dated January 18, 1945. I do not know why the reduction has been made. I can produce the original letter, if desired. I attach hereto a typed copy.

I have had experience in sheet metal fabrication, carpentry, painting and color mixing, cabinet making, and pattern making, and if assigned to shore duty could be useful in any of those branches, but in my present condition resulting from battle fatigue would ask not to be assigned to noisy sheet metal fabrication. In fact, I have had more experience in carpentry, painting, and color mixing. My broken ankle is still painful at times and makes me limp at times. I am now 36 years of age, having slightly fallen arches, a slight lordosis of the spine and have arthritis in my right thumb. These impairments are the result of my service in the U. S. Navy. I also have an offer of employment from the American Boat Works, 602 Northwest River Drive, Miami, for service in ship building, if discharged from naval service. In other words, I am capable of serviceable war industry ashore. I could also be of use in the rehabilitation services, teaching simple wood carving and designing.

Respectfully submitted

Hugh P. K. Corry

April 9, 1945

Hugh Corry's request for shore duty was followed by a medical exam, after which he was transferred to a hospital in Brooklyn New York, April 17, 1945. Treatment was completed September 26, 45, followed by an Honorable Discharge, "At the Convenience of the Government", presumably for a psychiatric disorder rendering him unfit for duty. Today we would call it PTSD. Corry was discharged from military service on 10/5/1945 in San Pedro, California. Having given his all to the war effort, losing a marriage, two brothers, and his sanity, his total separation pay was $168.94. He applied for a California State residency, a fact that followed him to his eventual burial in the Andersonville, Georgia military cemetery thirty-six years later. Does the California State residency keep Driftwood off South Carolina and Beaufort County records? There are no records in local census files, voting records, tax records, marriage records, or property records of any Hugh Patrick Knox Corry. He was never known to own or drive a car. Was this forensic invisibility by chance, or design?

The next six years of Corry's life are missing. This seems consistent with a pattern of constant moving and unrest, by products of the condition then known as Shell Shock, or today's PTSD.

We found record of Corry applying for a job as a painter's helper with the Chicago & Northwestern Railway Company on 4/12/1951. There again is no record of when he left that job, but deduction and timelines recounted by long time Beaufort natives may offer a clue.

Riding the rails across the Midwest and up and down the East Coast would have given Corry a road map to anywhere. This jives with a couple of locals remembering his arrival in the early '50's. I'm guessing Corry found that "End of the Road" place where he could hide out from whatever was chasing him, real or surreal. That place turned out to be Harbor Island, SC. A twenty-mile hike after jumping the train in Beaufort or Port Royal, SC would have been no problem for a man later known for his jaunty stride and regular walks to town from his Harbor Island driftwood shack. A 1954 Beaufort County Tax map aerial photo of Harbor Island shows Driftwood's shack "in situ" across the highway from the eventual site of the Johnson Creek Tavern Restaurant.

The tax map dating of Driftwood's arrival makes his age 57 when he got to Harbor Island. He probably quit-claimed the land he built his shack on.

There are several other ways Driftwood could have gotten to Beaufort. Never known to own a car makes that option unlikely. Hitch hiking, maybe? Or he could have crewed aboard a commercial freighter docking at Port Royal and jumped ship. With his naval history I would think he had had enough of sailing. Corry's certified history with the railroads gets my vote. Another "channeling moment" in that my fictional story has "Cory" hopping a train headed south to avoid the hangman's noose.

From that point forward began the twenty-year story of Driftwood Cory's time in Beaufort, from the late 1950's to the late 1970's, as fictionalized in "Driftwood Unmasked". Driftwood and his shack were island fixtures for a generation of surfers and beach goers heading to Hunting Island State Park. After his shack mysteriously burned down in 1963, Driftwood moved to the waterfront docks in Beaufort, picking up odd jobs here and there as a painter and furniture repair man. Wildly outlandish in every way, he was a character's character.

Anecdotal stories about Driftwood abound in the memories of Beaufort's older residents. Three come quickly to mind.

Wilson McIntosh, owner of The Beaufort Book Store, tells of a night when he saw Driftwood blowing fire from his mouth, as would a circus performer, the flames shooting clear across Bay Street, scaring the be-Jesus out of passersby. Driftwood wandered down a side street, flickering flames dancing off clabbered buildings, his howls of laughter melting away into the darkness.

Another tells of Driftwood getting a job at the Technical College of the Lowcountry, teaching pattern making and wood carving, only to soon be fired for groping a female teacher's derriere.

A shrimp boat captain once hired Driftwood and a helper to make repairs to his boat in dry dock. The captain gave Driftwood cash for the necessary materials. Returning late afternoon to inspect the work, he found Driftwood and helper drunk and passed out on the deck, amongst a pile of empty beer cans and liquor bottles and few repairs completed.

A regular at Ma Miller's Grocery store, Koth's Grocery, and The Yankee Bar & Grill swapping tall tales for booze, Driftwood left few footprints of his time in Beaufort. Unless you consider carvings, anecdotal stories, and his signature face carving on the palmetto tree in front of Ma Miller's aka/the Blood Bank building on Bellamy's Curve, Boundary Street. There are plans to preserve his palmetto time capsule, a footnote to Beaufort's colorful past and still more colorful characters.

When the real Hugh Patrick Knox Corry left town sometime in the late 1970's, why and how he ended up living out his last years in North Georgia remains a mystery. One of Beaufort's long-time residents that I interviewed offered that Driftwood had begun slipping into dementia, his wartime demons finally gaining the upper hand. The receipt of his death certificate from the Georgia Department of Vital Records shows Corry to have been an inpatient at the Veterans Administration Medical Center in Atlanta at the time of his death. My only conclusion is that some local agency must have arranged for the move to get Corry the medical attention he needed.

Corry died in Laurens, Georgia on 10/12/1981 at the age of 72. The death certificate listed no cause, no autopsy, no family or next of kin. A heroic and promising life broken by events he could not control, reduced to a single yellowed sheet of paper.

He was buried on 10/16/1981 in the Andersonville National Historical Site, Route 1, Box 800, Andersonville, GA, 31711, Section P, Site 778, S1C US Navy. His last known address was 31021, Dublin Street, Laurens, GA, USA.

Dublin Street? Really, how poetic is that?

So here we have it. The truth, Driftwood's redemption, my best efforts at finding the real Driftwood Cory; Hugh Patrick Knox Corry, Irish adventurer, sailor, painter, salesman, elevator operator, journalist, artist, charismatic story teller, decorated war veteran and beer drinker; carver of beautiful palmetto masks and totems, a peripheral visitor on the edge of reality, colorful, ratty, raucous, raunchy womanizer, unapologetically taunting social conformity; and an honorable man.

I believe Driftwood had a story to tell, and he chose me to tell it.

As the Gullah on the Island say, "We home, Driftwood..."

"...there is a little of Driftwood in each of us..."

Credits:

To Mary Ellen Thompson for her unwavering support for this project, for her editing, Gullah research, and storyline contributions.

To Maggie Shein for editing and sometimes painfully constructive criticism.

To Roger Pinckney XI for his anecdotal stories about Driftwood.

To Kathy Mascara for her photo of the real Driftwood, waterfront Beaufort, circa 1970.

To Linda Hawkins/Miller, David 'Hash' Brown, and Geddes Dowling for allowing me to photograph the palmetto totems and masks Driftwood gave them.

To Pamela Koth for the key to Driftwood's real-life story, turning the myth into the man.

To Hank Herring for creating the Mask, turning my imaginings into an artful reality.

To John Wollwerth, Wollwerth Imagery, for the cover photo.

To Grace Cordial of The Beaufort County Library and Beaufort Historic District for her bulldog tenacity in pulling Driftwood's life back from history's shadows into the light of redemption, restoring a little dignity to a man most assumed had none.

ABOUT THE AUTHOR

Photo Courtesy Wollwerth Imagery, Beaufort, SC
www.wollwerthimagery.com

Robert "Gibbes" McDowell, Jr. is a third-generation native son of Beaufort, South Carolina. His life credits include being a History Major, Retired Financial Planner, Collegiate and Masters Pole Vault Champion, and confirmed river rat-sportsman.

Author of numerous magazine articles published in *Professional Bowhunter Society, Bowhunter Magazine, Archery World,* and *Grey's Sporting Journal,* Gibbes was also co-producer of the acclaimed documentary *Sea Island Secrets* for South Carolina ETV. Three of his stories are included in Janet Garrity's *Fish Camps of the Sea Islands.*

Quite the athlete, Gibbes was featured on WCSC TV Channel 5 out of Charleston with sports clips of him doing interview and trick shooting. He was pole vault coach for Beaufort High School with five State titles (boys and girls) and has volunteered with Wild Turkey Foundation Women in the Outdoors as archery instructor and trick shooter, as well as Ducks Unlimited's Green Wing Youth Program.

While working on two other novels, in his free time you can find him shooting wild hogs with bow and arrows, tending to his fish camp, researching his story lines, and telling tall tales to anyone who wants to listen.

5-Star Review of "Driftwood Unmasked" by Joel R. Dennstedt
Readers' Favorite LLC

Sometimes, one comes upon such a unique piece of writing that he finds it difficult to categorize, but this also makes it equally memorable and appealing. Driftwood Unmasked by Gibbes McDowell is definitely fiction, but it is also self-admittedly based upon a real character existing in a real place and time. With an actual photograph of Driftwood Cory and some of his creative art to introduce and document the authentic fascination with such a "local character," the reader finds himself instantly intrigued and immediately drawn to a man with a very mysterious and unexplained past. Mr. McDowell, however, has done more than be intrigued; he has offered up a plausible if fictional account to explain this local legend of a man whose photograph radiates so much character that an historical account simply begs to be undertaken. Fortunately, Gibbes McDowell is the undaunted writer who chooses to reveal Driftwood Unmasked. One wonders if he might be channeling history's spirits in the process. With elegant and simple prose, a masterful accomplishment in itself, Mr. McDowell brings together a cast of fascinating characters, a background steeped in historical actuality, a series of mini-plots worthy of a great mystery writer, hidden treasure, and down-home southern island flavor only someone impeccably acquainted with the region could possibly express. That Driftwood Cory was an Irishman is the only spoiler this reviewer intends to tell, and that could easily be deduced from the photograph itself. How he became the local hermit creating memorable driftwood art is the story McDowell writes so well. He does honor to the best rumors and conjectures, and who knows, he may be telling the most accurate story of them all.

Coming Fall 2019

YELLOWSTONE

By

Gibbes McDowell